Catullan Questions

PRAECEPTORIBUS BALLIOLENSIBUS

Catullan Questions

T. P. Wiseman

Lecturer in Classics
University of Leicester

Leicester University Press
1969

First published in 1969 by
Leicester University Press

Distributed in North America by
Humanities Press Inc., New York

Copyright © T. P. Wiseman 1969

Set in Monotype Bembo
Printed in Great Britain by
Unwin Brothers Limited
The Gresham Press, Old Woking, Surrey

SBN 7185 1085 2

Contents

Acknowledgments

I am deeply indebted to Professor G. W. Williams for stimulating discussion of most of the points raised in this work. I am also very grateful to Mr R. G. C. Levens, Mr R. M. Ogilvie and Mr E. J. Phillips for helpful criticisms and comments on an earlier draft. But I have not always taken the advice so generously given—in particular, Gordon Williams will still groan at my views on poem 68—and I am alone responsible for the shortcomings of this book and the ideas expressed in it.

T. P. W.

List of Abbreviations

Works referred to by the author's name only:

K. Barwick, "Zyklen bei Martial und in den kleinen Gedichten des Catull", *Phil.* CII (1958) 284–318.

R. Ellis, *A Commentary on Catullus*, 2nd ed. (Oxford 1889).

L. Ferrero, *Interpretazione di Catullo* (Turin 1955).

C. J. Fordyce, *Catullus, a Commentary* (Oxford 1961).

E. Fraenkel, *Horace* (Oxford 1957).

W. Kroll, *Catull* (Stuttgart 1929).

P. Maas, "The Chronology of the Poems of Catullus", *CQ* XXXVI (1942) 79–82.

H. A. J. Munro, *Criticisms and Elucidations of Catullus* (London 1878).

K. Quinn, *The Catullan Revolution* (Melbourne 1959).

M. Rothstein, "Catull und Lesbia", *Phil.* LXXVIII (1923) 1–34.

E. Schäfer, *Das Verhaltnis von Erlebnis und Kunstgestalt bei Catull*, *Hermes* Einzelschriften, Heft 18 (Wiesbaden 1966).

A. L. Wheeler, *Catullus and the Traditions of Ancient Poetry*, Sather Classical Lectures, vol. 9 (Berkeley and Los Angeles 1934).

Periodicals, collections etc.:

AAT	*Atti della accademia delle scienze di Torino* (Turin).
AJP	*American Journal of Philology* (Baltimore).
Ath.	*Athenaeum* (Pavia).
Aumla	*Aumla*, Journal of the Australasian Universities Language and Literature Association (Christchurch, N.Z.).
CIG	*Corpus Inscriptionum Graecarum* (Berlin 1828–1877).
CIL	*Corpus Inscriptionum Latinarum* (Berlin 1862ff.).
CM	*Classica et Mediaevalia* (Copenhagen).
CP	*Classical Philology* (Chicago).

CQ	*The Classical Quarterly* (Oxford)
CR	*The Classical Review* (Oxford)
GIF	*Giornale italiano di filologia* (Naples).
Gl.	*Glotta* (Göttingen).
Gn.	*Gnomon* (Munich).
GR	*Greece and Rome* (Oxford)
Her.	*Hermes* (Wiesbaden).
Hist.	*Historia* (Wiesbaden).
HSCP	*Harvard Studies in Classical Philology* (Cambridge, Mass.).
ILLRP	*Inscriptiones Latinae Liberae Rei Publicae* (Florence 1957–1963).
JHS	*Journal of Hellenic Studies* (London).
JRS	*Journal of Roman Studies* (London).
Lat.	*Latomus* (Brussels).
NJKA	*Neue Jahrbücher für klassische Altertum* (Heidelberg).
Phil.	*Philologus* (Berlin and Wiesbaden).
PW	Paully-Wissowa, *Real-Encyclopädie der klassischen Altertumswissenschaft* (Stuttgart 1893ff.).
RFIC	*Rivista di filologia ed istruzione classica* (Turin).
RIGI	*Rivista indo-greca-italiana di filologia, lingua, antichità* (Naples).
RM	*Rheinisches Museum* (Frankfurt).
SEG	*Supplementum Epigraphicum Graecum* (Leiden).
TAPA	*Transactions of the American Philological Association* (Cornell).
TLL	*Thesaurus Linguae Latinae* (Leipzig 1900 ff.).
WS	*Wiener Studien* (Vienna).
YCS	*Yale Classical Studies* (New Haven).

PART ONE

I

THE PROBLEM

SIR RONALD SYME once described the chronology of Catullus' life and writings as "that imbroglio of problems where dogma and ingenuity have their habitation, where argument moves in circles, and no new passage in or out".[1] One of the most fundamental of the problems concerned is that of the arrangement of the poems: is it the work of the poet himself or of some subsequent compiler? The aim of this little book is to suggest that here, at least, with as little dogmatic ingenuity as possible, some new way in may be found, both enlightening for its own sake and useful for its relevance to Catullan chronology.

Ellis believed that the *libellus* dedicated by Catullus to Nepos in poem 1 was neither the collection as we have it (1–116) nor the first part of it (1–60), and that the ordering of the poems, though showing some evidence in places of deliberate arrangement, does not as it stands reflect the poet's own intention.[2] This last point was strongly upheld by Schmidt, to whom the arrangement as we have it appeared chaotic, in no order of subject-matter, feeling or chronology.[3] For Wilamowitz, on the other hand, there was no problem: "he arranged his book of poems with the most careful reflection (if anyone can't see it, *tant pis pour lui*)".[4] It would have been a help if the great man had given his reasons; but he did not, and most recent work in English has followed A. L. Wheeler, who in the first of his Sather lectures went back to Ellis' view: "the apparently purposed sequences are the exception, not the rule. The

[1] R. Syme, *CM* XVII (1956), 131.
[2] Ellis, pp. xlvi–l, 1–5.
[3] B. Schmidt, *RM* LXIX (1914), 278.
[4] U. von Wilamowitz-Moellendorff, *Sappho und Simonides* (Berlin 1913), 292.

rule in the detailed order of our collection is planlessness."[1] I believe that this is demonstrably false, and that Wilamowitz' dictum was justified.

The argument from absence of logical or chronological order cuts both ways: if Catullus himself could not have arranged his material so inconsequentially, why should any editor or compiler have done so?[2] Besides, it is possible that modern critics have been blinded to what Catullus was trying to do by their preoccupation with the "historical novel" element, the chronology of the poet's relationship with Lesbia.[3] There is in fact no reason to suppose that Catullus would choose to put his poems in chronological order. The nearest parallels in time are the early collections of Vergil and Horace: both the *Eclogues* and the first book of *Satires* are clearly not in chronological order of composition, but deliberately arranged by the poet to make a coherent artistic whole.[4] Unless we have good reason to believe otherwise, we may assume that Catullus did the same. Most modern scholars assume that the idea of a carefully arranged *libellus* did not occur to Roman poets before the Augustans,[5] but there is no basis for this supposition; indeed, a case can be made out for a deliberate arrangement in Lucilius, based on metrical variety.[6] Callimachus had arranged his *Iambics* (at least) in such a way as to achieve the maximum variety of metre, length, tone, subject-matter and dialect, and it is improbable that Catullus would have abandoned the Alexandrians' insistence on variation in all the aspects of poetic composition.[7]

So it is *a priori* more likely than not that Catullus arranged his collected poems with as much care as Vergil or Horace. What criterion did he use? Mette believes that 1–60, like some of Horace's *Odes*, were arranged metrically—in three roughly symmetrical

---

[1] Wheeler, pp. 26–9; Fordyce, p. 409.
[2] Cf. Quinn, p. 106 n. 11 on poems 1–60.
[3] On this tendency, see S. Commager, *HSCP* LXX (1965), 84. Cf. p. 34 n. 3 below.
[4] W. Port, *Phil.* LXXXI (1926), 280 ff., esp. 283–91; cf. Brooks Otis, *Virgil* (Oxford 1963), 128 ff. For the subject as a whole, see the bibliography in V. Buchheit, *Studien zum Corpus Priapeorum* (Munich 1962), 45 n. 3.
[5] E.g. B. Otis, *HSCP* LXX (1965), 38 (end of n. 8).
[6] See M. Puelma Piwonka, *Lucilius und Kallimachos* (Frankfurt 1949), 364–7.
[7] *Iambics:* C. M. Dawson, *YCS* XI (1950), 1–168, esp. 142–3. Hellenistic ποικιλία in general: L. Deubner, *NJKA* XLVII (1921), 361–78.

groups centred on 11, 31 and 51;[1] but this reconstruction is more ingenious than convincing, and involves at least one piece of special pleading (the inclusion of the Priapean fragment 1 as part of the first group). Mette relies on the precedent of Callimachus, which certainly implies that metre was an important factor, but since Callimachus sought other kinds of variety as well, it is surely misguided to abandon subject-matter as a criterion of arrangement.

A more promising approach is that of Barwick, who detected five cycles of poems, internally coherent and in a logical order.[2] Three of these cycles fall in the polymetric poems. The first consists of the Lesbia-poems 2, 3, 5, 7, 8 and 11: the first two poems clearly belong together at the untroubled beginning of the affair; the second two form an equally obvious diptych illustrating the height of the lovers' happiness;[3] 8 and 11 offer a sharp contrast in mood, with Catullus' backsliding resolve to end the affair and his final break with Lesbia. The arrangement clearly shows the beginning, fruition and end of Catullus' love for his mistress.[4]

The second cycle, concerning Aurelius, Furius and Juventius (15, 16, 21, 23, 24, 26), shows even more deliberate care: it is composed of two "triptychs" of three poems on Aurelius and Furius respectively, each separated after the first two of its three elements. 15 and 21 on Catullus' apprehension about Aurelius frame 16 on the *parum pudicus* polemic (which introduces Furius); 23 and 26 on Furius' poverty frame 24 on his attachment to Juventius.[5] This cycle also offers the readers an internally consistent "narrative" of Aurelius' and Furius' interest in Juventius, and Catullus' jealousy of them. The Veranius/Fabullus "cycle", however (9, 12, 13, 28, 47) is less obviously in a logical order—perhaps merely because here there is no "plot"—and much less tightly-knit. Barwick's theory

---

[1] H. J. Mette, *Gn.* XXVIII (1956), 35–6. See E. C. Wickham, *The Works of Horace*, I (Oxford 1896), 25–30 on variety of metre, subject and tone in the *Odes*.

[2] Barwick, pp. 312–18.

[3] But Barwick does not observe the development from 5 ("we") to 7 ("you" and "I"); cf. Ferrero, pp. 173–4 on the more careful construction of 7.

[4] Cf. Commager, *loc. cit.* (p. 2 n. 3 above), 102 on cross-references within the cycle: *soles* in 5.4/8.3,8, *vivere* in 5.1/11.17 (both relevant to 3.11 ff.?). See now the interesting article of C. P. Segal on the order of poems 2–11, in *Lat.* XXVI (1968), 305–21, which appeared too late for me to make use of his arguments.

[5] Barwick, p. 315. Cross-references: 21.2–3/24.2–3, 21.1/23.14, 23.1/24.5, 16.1/21.8,13, etc.

does not explain why 28 and 47 are separated from the other poems and from each other; nor does he offer any general explanation of the juxtaposition or separation of the poems in each group,[1] or account for the arrangement of the poems not included in these cycles.

Before we try to pursue Barwick's idea and look for a more all-embracing principle of arrangement, it is worth considering some of the ways and means open to a poet arranging his work for publication, faced with the problem of imposing a unified system or a logical order on a collection of heterogeneous short poems originally written for different occasions, in different styles and on different subjects.

He might create a simple pattern by grouping together poems of similar theme, tone or metre. A poet with the Alexandrian ideal of variation in mind, however, would not be satisfied with simply isolating groups or cycles of related poems placed in sequence; but the more complex an arrangement he made, for instance by interlocking different themes or deliberately interrupting his groups of poems for a specific effect, the more progressively difficult his task would become. There would always be a build-up of individual poems which did not obviously belong in any series, with the inevitable result that the complexity of the arrangement would have to be relaxed to fit them in.

The poet could also write new material which would make the connections of thought or theme within the collection more obvious or improve its proportions.[2] He could even indicate more or less explicitly to the reader what to expect next, as Callimachus had done in the epilogue to the *Aitia*—though whether αὐτὰρ ἐγὼ Μουσέων πεζὸν ἔπειμι νομόν indicates a change to prose or to satirical verse is in dispute.[3] Such programme-poems are often found at the beginning of ancient verse-collections, and Catullus' own dedicatory first poem fulfils this function, among others;[4] but they might

---

[1] E.g.: why is 7 next to 8, but 8 and 11 separated by two poems?

[2] Cf. Fraenkel, p. 124; exemplified by Hor. *epod.* 3, *Sat.* I 1, II 1, *Odes* I 1 (Fraenkel, pp. 69, 96, 230).

[3] Call. fr. 112.9 Pf; R. Pfeiffer, *Callimachus* II (Oxford 1953), xxxvi, and Dawson, *op. cit.* (p. 2 n. 7 above), 146–8. Cf. Fraenkel, p. 262.

[4] E.g. Martial I pref., V 2, XI 2, *Priapea* 1–2. On "lepidum novum libellum", programmatic as well as descriptive, see F. O. Copley, *TAPA* LXXXII (1951), 201–2, and now also J. P. Elder, *HSCP* LXXI (1966), 143–9 (who I think is too subtle).

also be placed in the middle of a collection to indicate a change of subject, like Martial III 68 (cf. 86), which announces to his female readers the increased *impudicitia* of the rest of the book.

Any collection of "occasional" poems might include some written with a particular recipient in mind, though not necessarily (if ever) for his eyes only.[1] The collection itself, however, must be aimed at "the reader", an unknown person presumably unfamiliar with the original circumstances out of which the poem grew. What was obvious for the recipient of the poem might need illumination for the reader of the collection; on the other hand, the poet could now abandon the original context of a poem if he wanted to use it for a particular "structural" purpose in the arrangement. (As a crude example, a love poem written to or about Madame A, but without naming her, could be included in a cycle of poems celebrating Madame B.) In arranging the collection, the poet must have his reader in mind throughout. Since all the reader knows of the poet's world is what he infers from the poems, they must be so placed as to give him a reasonably intelligible picture, becoming more detailed as he progresses. The picture need not be true, of course; the poet is not obliged to provide an autobiography, and even if each individual poem reflected a part of his experience with the minimum of artistic distortion, their order and juxtaposition might still give the reader a quite different idea of it. The "world of the poems" has only to be self-consistent and intelligible.[2]

How easily intelligible the poet makes it depends on how literate and sophisticated a reader he is aiming at. If he writes for his fellow-poets, or an audience familiar with poetic technique and prepared to listen for nuances and overtones, the signposts he uses to indicate the pattern of the collection need not be obvious at the first reading, or detectable at all by those who do not know what to look for. In Catullus' case, both the Alexandrian and the Roman poetic traditions on which he drew presupposed a small, learned and discriminating readership prepared to judge the poet as he would judge himself: Callimachus' first *Iambic* implies an audience of *philologoi*, while Lucilius (like Horace after him) made it clear that

---

[1] For Cat. 50, a strictly "occasional" poem but written with other readers in mind, see Fraenkel, p. 314.

[2] Cf. Ovid *am.* III 12.19: "nec tamen ut testes mos est audire poetas".

he was writing for "pauci et sapientes".[1] Catullus' sneer at the crude taste of the *populus* in poem 95 shows clearly enough that he thought his own work belonged to that category which "does not fear the critic's keen perception and continues to please at the tenth reading".[2] So we need not expect a simple or obvious arrangement of his poems, nor indications explicit enough for any *caprimulgus aut fossor* (22.10) to understand.

It is important to remember this point, since the principle of Catullus' arrangement argued below depends (for the first sixty poems at any rate) on the identification of two programme poems which are by no means recognizable as such at first sight.

---

[1] Call. fr. 191 Pf (with *Dieg.* VI 2); Luc. 461, 687 M, cf. Hor. *Sat.* I 4.73, 10.74 and 87, *Ep.* I 20.3 f.

[2] Hor. *AP* 364–5; Cat. 95.10. Cf. Quinn, p. 68 on Catullus' discriminating readers; Fraenkel, p. 124f on the self-consciousness of Latin poetry in general.

See Pindar *Ol.* 2.83–6 for "hard" poetry which is only clear τοῖς συνετοῖσιν: the quotation is used by David West as an epigraph to ch. 9 of his *Reading Horace* (Edinburgh 1967), a book which contains many observations and examples relevant to this chapter (*e.g.* pp. 26–7 on Hor. *Ep.* I 13).

II

THE POLYMETRIC SHORT POEMS (1–60)

The tripartite division

> Si qui forte mearum ineptiarum
> lectores eritis manusque vestras
> non horrebitis admovere nobis . . . (14a)

IF only this poem had survived complete, Catullus' arrangement
would no doubt present no problems. As it is, the fragment has
been interpreted as the remains of an epilogue or the dedication
of another *libellus*, and thus as strong evidence against the collection
as we have it being the poet's own arrangement.[1] But why should
Catullus' readers *shrink* from touching his book? The language
seems too strong for mere modest deprecation. However, when we
consider that the cycle of poems on Aurelius, Furius and Juventius
begins immediately afterwards, it becomes intelligible as part of a
warning to the reader that poems of an avowedly homosexual
nature follow.[2]

> Minister vetuli puer Falerni,
> inger mi calices amariores,
> ut lex Postumiae iubet magistrae
> ebrioso acino ebriosioris.
> At vos quo lubet hinc abite, lymphae,
> vini pernicies, et ad severos
> migrate. Hic merus est Thyonianus. (27)

This poem is complete, but apparently pointless.[3] It also contains
a difficulty which has never been satisfactorily explained: why
should the slave pour out *bitterer* wine? The supposedly parallel
passage from Seneca quoted by Kroll and Fordyce is not really

[1] See Ellis, p. 4; Wheeler, p. 221.
[2] On the need for warning (or apology), see G. W. Williams, *JRS* LII (1962), 39–40.
[3] Cf. J. D. P. Bolton, *CR* XVII (1967), 12, on "the joke, such as it is".

B

convincing, since Seneca was maintaining a paradox, that unpleasant things can be enjoyable, and cannot be taken to prove that *amaritudo* was considered a virtue in wine.[1] It was, however, considered a virtue in satirical poetry—the word is practically a literary technical term for invective[2]—and the image of poets and non-poets as wine-drinkers and water-drinkers has a long history in ancient literature.[3] So perhaps the real subject of the poem is poetry, and its real purpose to announce a vein of invective in the collection—which follows in the next two poems.

Recognition of this may help to explain the name "Thyonianus" in the last line, if it was chosen to remind the reader of the Greek verb θύειν —"now for the real savage stuff".[4] Much more important, I believe it enables us to see a fundamental threefold division in the 1–60 collection: the Lesbia-cycle, the Juventius-cycle, and the invective poems.

In the first column (*a*) of Table I, I have set out the poems by subject-matter, using these three categories (abbreviated as L, J and I);[5] it will be seen at once that they do not at first overlap, and that they have quite clearly defined beginnings at poems 2, 15 and 28—i.e., after the dedication and the two poems discussed above. This would seem to confirm the identification of 14a and 27 as programme poems; in which case, not only do we disarm one of the main arguments of the "late-compiler" school of thought (on the purpose of 14a), but we have to suppose that Catullus wrote these poems deliberately for this function, and for the positions in the collection which they in fact occupy.

The second column (*b*) of Table I may illustrate an internal metrical scheme designed to give variation in metre as well as subject-matter. The succession of six hendecasyllabic poems from

---

[1] Sen. *ep.* 63.5; Kroll, p. 50; Fordyce, p. 157.

[2] *TLL* I 1817.70 ff., 1818.62 ff., 1822.21 ff. E.g.: Pliny *NH* XXXVI 12 (Hipponax) Val. Max. IX 1. ext. 6, Porph. on Hor. *Odes* IV 9.7 (Alcaeus), Tac. *dial.* 25 (Caelius Rufus).

[3] Fraenkel, p. 340 on Hor. *Ep.* I 19.3 and Cratinus, etc. Note the similarity of 27.5 to 14.21 and 36.18, also about poetry.

[4] Cf. Hor. *Odes* I 17.23 ("Thyoneus" in the context of *proelia*). I wonder, too, whether "vetuli Falerni" in line I would make a literate Roman think of Lucilius, whose home was Suessa Aurunca next to the *ager Falernus*: see Hor. *Sat.* II 1.34 (cf I 10.67, *Ep.* II 1.56, Persius I 123), for Lucilius *senex*.

[5] For the difficulty of isolating categories, cf. Quinn, p. 37 on "levels of intent".

12 to 16 is broken by the beginning of a new section at 14a; in the longer third section, it is true that we have two sequences of six and seven poems in the same metre (45–50; 53–58a), but the second of these is in fact broken by the experimental "spondaic" rhythm of 55. Perhaps, we may say that a presumed aim of metrical variation may be inferred from the idea of a new cycle beginning at 14a.

If this is so, of course, we have to explain (or somehow punctuate) the sequence of hendecasyllables at 45–50. We have also still to account for the overlapping of the first and second groups of poems with the third—i.e., the presence of several Lesbia-poems and one on Juventius (48) *after* the announcement of the "invective" theme. Finally, we must try to explain the arrangement of the poems which do not fall into any of our three categories but which interrupt and separate those that do (the "occasional" poems, for want of a more precise term).[1]

Arrangement of the first two parts

One point relevant to the arrangement of the earlier occasional poems is the *lepor* of Catullus' work announced in the first poem.[2] The key words *lepidus, salsus, venustus, facetus* (and their opposites), which embody the social and literary ideals of the poet and his friends, have a curiously unbalanced distribution in our collection of Catullus' poems: nearly 60 per cent of their occurrences fall in the first twenty-five poems.[3] Of the occasional pieces which punctuate the Lesbia- and Juventius-cycles of our first two groups, poems 6, 10, 12, 17, 22 and 25 can be taken as illustrations of social *ineptiae*, unacceptable behaviour which has the effect of emphasizing by contrast the *lepor* of the poet himself and his close friends:[4]

---

[1] i.e., nos. 4, 6, 9, 10, 12, 13, 14, 17, 22, 25, 31, 32, 34, 35, 38?, 40?, 44, 45, 46, 49, 50, 53, 55, 56, 58a, 59, 60?. One of them (poem 31, the first non-invective after poem 27) may also be explained metrically: it is in choliambics, a metre traditionally associated with satirical poems, though the subject-matter is thoroughly non-satirical.

[2] P. 4 n. 4 above.

[3] *Lepor, (il)lepidus:* 1.1, 6.2, 17, 10.4, 12.8, 16.7; 32.2, 36.10,17, 50.7, 78.1–2. *Facetiae, (in)facetus:* 12.9, 22.14; 36.19, 43.8, 50.8. *(In)venustus:* 3.2, 10.4, 12.5, 13.6, 22.2; 31.12, 35.17, 36.17, 86.3, 89.2, 97.9. *Sal(sus), insulsus:* 10.33, 12.4, 13.5, (14.16?), 16.7, 17.2; 37.6, 86.4. *Ineptus, ineptiae:* 6.14, 8.1, 12.4, 14a.1, 17.12, 25.8; 39.16. Total in 1–25: 24/25 out of 41/42.

[4] 6.17, 12.8–9; add 13.7, which belongs next to 12 because of its subject-matter and its addressee (Barwick, p. 316).

TABLE I

	a (subject)	*b* (metre)	*c* (place-names)
1. Cui dono lepidum novum libellum	L	h	
2. Passer, deliciae meae puellae	L	h	
2a. (Tam gratum est mihi quam ferunt puellae)		h	
3. Lugete, o Veneres Cupidinesque	L	h	
4. Phaselus ille quem videtis, hospites	L	i	Adriatic, Cyclades, etc.
5. Vivamus, mea Lesbia, atque amemus	L	h	
6. Flavi, delicias tuas Catullo	L	h	(Syrian perfume)
7. Quaeris quot mihi basiationes	L	h	(Libya, Cyrene)
8. Miser Catulle, desinas ineptire	L	c	
9. Verani, omnibus e meis amicis		h	Spain
10. Varus me meus ad suos amores		h	Bithynia
11. Furi et Aureli, comites Catulli	L	s	India, Parthia, etc.
12. Marrucine Asini, manu sinistra		h	Spain
13. Cenabis bene, mi Fabulle, apud me		h	
14. Ni te plus oculis meis amarem		h	
14a. (Siqui forte mearum ineptiarum)		h	
15. Commendo tibi me ac meos amores	J	h	
16. Pedicabo ego vos et irrumabo	J	h	
17. O Colonia, quae cupis ponte ludere longo	J	p	(Colonia)
21. Aureli pater esuritionum	J	h	
22. Suffenus iste, Vare, quem probe nosti	J	c	
23. Furi, cui neque servus est neque arca	J	h	
24. O qui flosculus es Iuventiorum	J	h	
25. Cinaede Thalle, mollior cuniculi capillo	J	i	(Bithynia, Spain)
26. Furi, villula vostra non ad Austri	J	h	
27. Minister vetuli puer Falerni		h	
28. Pisonis comites, cohors inanis	I	h	(Spain, Bithynia?)

No.	First line					
29.	Quis hoc potest videre, quis potest pati		I		i	Gaul, Britain, etc.
30.	Alfene immemor atque unanimis false sodalibus		(I)	c	a	
31.	Paene insularum Sirmio insularumque			h		Sirmio, Bithynia
32.	Amabo, mea dulcis Ipsitilla		I	h		
33.	O furum optime balneariorum					
34.	Dianae sumus in fide				g	(Delos)
35.	Poetae tenero, meo sodali	(L)	I	h		Novum Comum
36.	Annales Volusi, cacata charta	(L)	I	h		Idalium, Urii, etc.
37.	Salax taberna vosque contubernales	(L)		c		Spain
38.	Malest, Cornifici, tuo Catullo		I			
39.	Egnatius, quod candidos habet dentes	(L)		c		Spain (Sabina, etc.)
40.	Quaenam te mala mens, miselle Ravide		I	h		
41.	Ameana puella defututa		I	h		Formiae
42.	Adeste, hendecasyllabi quot estis	(L)	(I)	h		(Gaul)
43.	Salve, nec minimo puella naso			h		Formiae (Cis. Gaul)
44.	O funde noster seu Sabine seu Tibur			c		Sabina, Tibur
45.	Acmen Septimius suos amores			h		(Libya, India, etc.)
46.	Iam ver egelidos refert tepores			h		Bithynia, Asia
47.	Porci et Socration, duae sinistrae	J		h		(Spain?)
48.	Mellitos oculos tuos, Iuventi			h		
49.	Disertissime Romuli nepotum			h		
50.	Hesterno, Licini, die otiosi	L				
51.	Ille mi par esse deo videtur				s	
52.	Quid est, Catulle? Quid moraris emori?		I		i	
53.	Risi nescioquem modo e corona			h		
54.	Othonis caput oppido est pusillum		I	h		
55.	Oramus, si forte non molestum est			(h)		
56.	O rem ridiculam, Cato, et iocosam			h		
57.	Pulcre convenit improbis cinaedis		I	h		(Formiae)
58.	Caeli, Lesbia nostra, Lesbia illa	L		h		
58a.	Non custos si fingar ille Cretum			h		
59.	Bononiensis Rufa Rufulum fellat			c		(Bononia)
60.	Num te leaena montibus Libystinis	(L)		c		(Libya)

hoc salsum esse putas? fugit te, inepte:
quamvis sordida res et invenusta est.   (12.4–5)

But *lepidus* was a literary as well as a social compliment, and Catullus' self-advertisement in 1.1 is also picked up in the early poems by the promise of *lepidus versus* at 6.17 and the examples of what *not* to write in 14 and 22. The poet's self-defence against the criticisms of Furius and Aurelius in poem 16 is also relevant here, for its explanation of how poems gain "sal ac leporem"; so too is the reference to Battus' tomb, surely a deliberate reminder of Callimachus, in the seventh poem.[1] However, both of these pieces are placed primarily as units in the Juventius- and Lesbia-cycles.

In fact, the two cycles and the occasional poems which interrupt them are cunningly intertwined in several different ways.[2] Apart from the literary references in 7 and 16, we find the "ineptus" idea in the first line of poem 8 on Lesbia and in the programmatic poem 14a; poems 6 and 10 on *scorta* are placed among the Lesbia-poems while 25 ("Cinaede Thalle . . .") is appropriately situated in the homosexual Furius/Aurelius/Juventius group;[3] poems 17 and 22, on men who were unaware of their own faults,[4] punctuate the closely-knit groups of poems on two men who were themselves *impudici*, but accused Catullus of their own vice.[5]

Moreover, T. E. Kinsey has recently pointed out that the theme of foreign travel in the first three stanzas of 11 has been prepared for by the previous poem on Catullus' mythical Bithynian bearers, which itself (as Ferrero observed) is relevant to poem 9 on Veranius' happy return from Spain, and doubtless placed deliberately next to

---

[1] 16.7; 7.6, on which see K. F. Quinn, in *Critical Essays on Roman Literature, Elegy and Lyric* (ed. J. P. Sullivan, London 1962), 42. Cf. 10.26 on the *Alexandrian* god Sarapis.

[2] The two cycles themselves are connected by poems 11 (Furius and Aurelius) and 16 (cross-reference to 5.7 ff. and 7.9 in line 12). Poem 22 on Suffenus picks up 14.19, and the Spanish napkins of 12.14 reappear in 25.7.

[3] The *mollitia* of Thallus (25.1, 10) reminds one of 16.4 & 8, and contrasts with the desiccated Furius of poem 23.

[4] 17.22, 22.17–21. Suffenus, like Furius, is a *homo bellus* (22.9, 24.7); it is conceivable that "caprimulgus aut fossor" at 22.10 had homosexual connotations (see 80.8 for *mulgere*, Juv. II 10 for *fossa*); and the Priapean metre of 17 may have been a reason for the poem's inclusion at this point.

[5] 16.4; cf. Schäfer, pp. 26–7 for the ironical emphasis on *pudicitia* in these poems (15.2, 5, 13; 21.12).

it.[1] I would go further, and suggest that poems 4, 9, 10 and 12 were placed in this order to give the reader a coherently developing picture of Catullus' travels and those of his friends: "The owner of the *phaselus* was in Bithynia (4); Veranius was in Spain (9); I was in Bithynia (so the *phaselus* was mine)[2] (10); Fabullus was with Veranius in Spain (12)." We then continue with Fabullus in poem 13, where the empty wallet of line 8 is surely a reminder of 10.9 ff. on the unprofitableness of Bithynia.[3] If this reconstruction is justified, then poem 11 fulfils at least three "structural" purposes, in picking up the theme of travel, in crowning the Lesbia-cycle, and in introducing the reader to the men who feature with Juventius in the following group.[4]

I conclude, then, that the first 26 poems in our collection were carefully arranged around the framework of the two cycles on Lesbia and Juventius, the intervening occasional poems being placed to achieve the maximum variation of both metre and subject-matter, while still offering the reader a coherent development of the themes of *lepor/ineptiae* and foreign travel. Can an equally careful arrangement be detected in poems 27–60?

Arrangement of the third part

Here we must put ourselves in the poet's position, and remember one of the problems mentioned in the first chapter: the subtle and manifold arrangement of the first 26 poems cannot be kept up throughout the collection, simply because of the inevitable piling-up of poems which do not obviously belong in any sequence but which must be fitted in somewhere. The criteria for arranging them thus become less easily detectable, being (as the absence of programme poems after 27 shows) for the poet's own convenience rather than the guidance of the reader. We should also bear in mind that the tight construction of the earlier cycles might have meant

[1] T. E. Kinsey, *Lat.* XXIV (1965), 540; Ferrero, p. 221. See Fraenkel, pp. 429–30 for observations relevant to the "loca facta nationes" of 9.7.

[2] Whether it was really his (M. C. J. Putnam, *CP* LVII (1962), 10–19, *contra* F. O. Copley, *TAPA* LXXXIX (1958), 9–13) is beside the point; what matters is that the reader is meant to infer that it was.

[3] There may also be a play on *beatiorem* in poem 9 and 10.17: "Veranius is back from Spain, I'm lucky; I'm back from Bithynia, I wasn't lucky."

[4] Cf. Ferrero, p. 258, on the irony of "comites Catulli"—the reader soon realizes they are being given a dirty job.

that some poems relevant to Lesbia and Juventius could not be used there, and must be inserted somewhere else; we should therefore not be surprised to find Lesbia-poems among the occasional pieces which separate the invectives of the third group (introduced by poem 27). Having read poems 2–11, the reader is immediately able to place each of them in its context.[1] With this in mind, we can now attempt to make sense of poems 27–60.

The third column (c) in Table I sums up what I take to be an important factor: the occurrence of place-names, which indicates (I think) a return to the "foreign travel" theme of the first cycle (poems 4–12). But the place-names noticeably preponderate in the first half of the third group, from 28 to 47—and both these two poems are about the unfortunate *cohors* of Piso. Could it be that 28–47 form a unit beginning and ending with (Memmius and) Piso, continuing the theme of foreign travel but with the added *amaritudo* forecast in poem 27? If so, the problem of the six consecutive hendecasyllable poems from 45 to 50 would be solved (the end of the hypothetical 28–47 sequence would split them neatly in two), and poem 48 on Juventius could be taken as announcing a return to homosexual themes in the occasional poems of the remainder of the collection.[2]

Considered as a unit, the sequence 28–47 displays other possible symmetries besides the two Piso poems: for instance, 31 on the return from Bithynia to Sirmio (in scazons) might balance 44 on the Sabine farm (also in scazons) and 46 on the departure from Bithynia. More important, I think, is the group of five poems in the middle of this putative sequence (36–40), which depends on the interpretation of 38. I follow Kroll in believing that Catullus is asking Cornificius for a poem to cure his love-sickness, as Mallius asked Catullus in 68.10[3]—and, in particular, a poem in elegiacs, the "sad" metre

---

[1] Perhaps the same applies to Juventius—but see below on the possible significance of poem 48.

[2] i.e. 55 and 58a on Camerius, 56 on the *pupulus*. Poem 50 to Calvus might also qualify by its quasi-erotic vocabulary; the poem *could* be understood in a homosexual context. See T. E. Kinsey, *Lat.* XXV (1966), 106, though I do not agree with his main point.

[3] Kroll, pp. 71–2. Cf. F. O. Copley, *TAPA* LXXXVII (1956), 125 ff., who rightly insists that the key to the poem must be within it; however, he sees it in the name of Simonides rather than that of Cornificius, who would be known to Catullus' readers as a poet.

par excellence,[1] as well as that appropriate to Catullus' plight. I should therefore take line 6 to mean "is this all you think of my unhappy love-affairs?", and *meos amores* to refer, as in 40.7, to Lesbia. If this is so, then all five poems are concerned with Lesbia, though less directly than the poems of the first cycle—here she is in the background, and the reader's attention is rather on Volusius' *Annals*, the *salax taberna* and its inmates, and Cornificius, Egnatius and Ravidus. On each side of this group, poem 35 possibly balances 41 and 43: "my friend Caecilius lives in Comum, and his girl-friend is a good critic—my enemy Mamurra lives in Formiae, and his girl-friend is an ugly slut".

As for 48–60, they contain not only the first homosexual poems since no. 25, but also the first political poems since no. 29 (unless poem 49 on Cicero counts), in the sequence 52–54. These three short pieces follow poem 50 on the *otiosi* Catullus and Calvus, and the adaptation from Sappho (51) which ends with the poet's reflection that *otium* has destroyed him:[2] could it be that this stanza marks a farewell to *otium* (and love), and that it is for this reason that the following poems return to politics (*negotia*)?

Other even more tenuous hints could be found which *might* correspond with Catullus' private design, but such speculation is fruitless; what matters is what the poet meant the *reader* to be conscious of. Here I think we can fairly claim that in the first half of the invective group announced at poem 27 (i.e. 28–47), the reader feels he is taken far afield, not only to Sirmio, Comum and various parts of Italy (cf. 39), but to Spain, Gaul, Britain and the East, and he is left in little doubt of the profitlessness of such adventuring; it is good to get back, and better still never to go at all, but stay at home and make love like Acme and Septimius. In the second half (48–60) he returns to Rome, where Cicero is *omnium patronus*, where Vatinius swears by his consulate and Calvus reels off his crimes in the Forum, where Camerius lurks among the light ladies of Pompey's colonnade—and where Lesbia now haunts the alleys and street-corners with the great-hearted sons of Remus.[3] The

---

[1] Catullus would, of course, be as well aware of the ἔλεγος—ἐλεγεῖα etymology as Horace or Ovid—*Odes* I 33.3 (significantly about a faithless mistress), *Amores* III 9.3, *Her.* XV 7–8. See also p. 18 below (and Schäfer, pp. 46–7) on poem 65.

[2] See further p. 33 f. below on poem 51.

[3] 49, 52, 53, 55, 58; note also 57.4, "*urbana altera et illa Formiana*".

sudden change of scene is very noticeable: so perhaps Catullus *did* make a deliberate break in his third group of poems, between 47 and 48.

It is surely significant that the hideous picture of Lesbia in poem 58 comes almost at the end of a collection which began with the sparrow-poems. Moreover, though the final poem in the 1–60 collection may seem vague, inconclusive and unsatisfactory to modern taste, a contemporary reader would rightly have recognized it as a bitter address to the mistress whose pet began the collection and whom the poet throughout has not allowed us to forget.[1] The reader is meant to realize that the first three lines allude to Jason's complaint to Medea and are therefore addressed by a lover to a cruel woman;[2] the Libyan lioness of line 1 might remind him of the Libyan sands of poem 7,[3] and the reference to Scylla's *inguina* (not, so far as we know, a traditional part of the simile) would surely put him in mind of the insultingly physical way in which the poet describes Lesbia's activities in 11.20, 37.14 and 58.5.[4] So poem 60 both concludes the "calices amariores" of the third main theme announced by Catullus (along with 59, it forms the only non-separated pair of poems in the satirical choliambic metre), and seals the 1–60 collection as a whole in a poem which sums up its nature—literate and allusive, elegant but passionate, and with more than a dash of Hipponactean bitterness.

[1] On this poem see O. Weinreich, *Her.* LXXXVII (1959), 75 ff., esp. 78–84—though I do not agree with his theory of the interconnection of poems 58–60. Against Weinreich, Schäfer (pp. 63–7) rightly points out that the language of 60 is more reminiscent of poems 30, 71, 73 and 104 than of the Lesbia-poems; but whatever the poem's original context, its position in the collection makes the reader think of poem 58 and Lesbia, not poem 30 and Alfenus.

[2] Eur. *Med.* 1341–3, cf. 1358–9. Weinreich, *loc. cit.* 84 for later uses of the theme, all with reference to lovers.

[3] And of the angry Dionysus' destruction of Pentheus (Eur. *Bacch.* 988 ff.)? Libyan lions also appear at 45.6–7.

[4] So Ferrero, pp. 190 f.; cf. N. J. Herescu, *Gl.* XXXVIII (1959), 125 ff. for poem 37. Weinreich (*loc. cit.* 89–90) takes the collocation of 59 and 60 as reflecting unkindly on Lesbia.

III

THE LONG POEMS AND THE EPIGRAMS
(61–116)

Poem 65

> Etsi me assiduo confectum cura dolore
>   seuocat a doctis, Ortale, uirginibus,
> nec potis est dulcis Musarum expromere fetus
>   mens animi, tantis fluctuat ipsa malis—
> namque mei nuper Lethaeo gurgite fratris
>   pallidulum manans alluit unda pedem,
> Troia Rhoeteo quem subter litore tellus
>   ereptum nostris obterit ex oculis.
>
> . . . .
>
> numquam ego te, uita frater amabilior,   10
> aspiciam posthac? at certe semper amabo,
>   semper maesta tua carmina morte canam,
> qualia sub densis ramorum concinit umbris
>   Daulias, absumpti fata gemens Ityli—
> sed tamen in tantis maeroribus, Ortale, mitto
>   haec expressa tibi carmina Battiadae,
> ne tua dicta uagis nequiquam credita uentis
>   effluxisse meo forte putes animo,
> ut missum sponsi furtiuo munere malum
>   procurrit casto uirginis e gremio,   20
> quod miserae oblitae molli sub ueste locatum,
>   dum aduentu matris prosilit, excutitur,
> atque illud prono praeceps agitur decursu,
>   huic manat tristi conscius ore rubor.

THE twelfth line of this poem is the only passage in our collection of Catullus' poems with an apparently explicit programmatic content: addressing his dead brother, the poet promises "semper maesta tua carmina morte canam".[1] Is this

---

[1] On the Veronensis' reading *tegam*, the last word was said by Munro, p. 155.

meant to be taken seriously? It is true that all the other references to Catullus' brother come *after* this (68.19 ff. and 91 ff.; 101); it is also true that the two passages in 68, at least, seem to refer to the death with an abruptness which might imply that the reader was expected to know about it—as opposed to poem 65, where he is left to gather what has happened gradually, as he reads lines 5–9. But what about "semper"? Neither the *Coma Berenices* nor poem 67 is even remotely relevant to the brother's death,[1] and only one (101) of the short poems from 69 to 116 is concerned with the subject announced in 65. The point is, I think, that *tua morte* goes with *maesta*:[2] "I shall (from now on) always write poems which are *maesta* because of your death." The promise is not to keep writing about the brother's death, but to keep writing *carmina maesta*—which means, if our previous analysis of poem 38 was correct (p. 14 above), to keep writing elegiacs. And, of course, the rest of our collection *is* in elegiacs.

But there is more in poem 65 than this. It is an excellent example of Catullus' allusive technique, and of the demands he makes on his reader. In the very last line, for example, by his use, for the second time in the poem, of the verb *manare*, he sends the reader back to line 6 to pick up the contrast between the corpse's pale foot and the girl's red face—and to recall, perhaps, the fruit of the virgin Muses and the water of oblivion (lines 2–3; 5) in the light of the chaste girl's apple and the forgetfulness with which she drops it (19–20, 21).[3] As for allusiveness, the simile at lines 13–14 refers the literate reader straight to Homer (*Odyssey* XIX 518 ff.), both by the name-form Itylus, rather than the usual Itys, and by the quotation of "sub densis ramorum . . . umbris" from Homer's δενδρέων ἐν πετάλοισι . . . πυκινοῖσιν; thus it adds the picture of Penelope's sleepless grief for Odysseus to the poet's own mourning for his brother.

But there is a curious problem in this simile: Homer's Itylus is the son of the Theban king Zethus and Aëdon, accidentally killed by his mother, who was transformed into a nightingale. Catullus, on the other hand, makes him the son of the Thracian Tereus, king of Daulis, and Procne—the "Daulian bird" of 65.14—who kills him and serves him up to Tereus in revenge for the latter's rape and

---

[1] Despite Ferrero (p. 98) on 66.22 "fratris cari flebile discidium".

[2] So Ellis, *ad loc.*; Fordyce takes it with *canam*, Kroll admits either possibility.

[3] For this sort of construction, see Schäfer, p. 24 on poem 99.

mutilation of her sister Philomela; Procne, like Aëdon in the other story, becomes a nightingale, Philomela a swallow. The Procne legend is much more common than the one referred to in Homer; but Procne's son is universally called Itys, not Itylus. Why does Catullus, by his clear reference to Homer and the Aëdon legend and by putting *Daulias* (i.e. Procne) in the most emphatic position, so explicitly confuse the two stories? In a poem manifestly composed with great care and attention to detail, such an apparent anomaly must mean something.

I suggest that by calling attention to the name Daulias in line 14, Catullus wants to refer his readers particularly to the story of Procne and Tereus, and the treatment of it by the Alexandrian poets. It is, of course, hazardous to argue about hypothetical references to a literature which is almost completely lost; but we can infer something of the Alexandrians' work from Ovid's *Metamorphoses* and Nonnus' *Dionysiaca*, both of which were largely based on it. In this particular case, it is possible that one important element of the Hellenistic version of the story has survived in both works: compare the beginning of Ovid's long narrative (*Met.* VI 426–674), on Procne's marriage to Tereus:

> non pronuba Iuno,
> non Hymenaeus adest, non illi Gratia lecto;
> Eumenides tenuere faces de funere raptos,
> Eumenides stravere torum, tectoque profanus
> incubuit bubo thalamique in culmine sedit.
> Hac ave coniuncti Procne Tereusque, parentes
> hac ave sunt facti

with Nonnus' brief digression from his story of Cadmus to tell of the rape of Philomela:

> Δαυλίδος ἔστιχεν οὖδας ὁμούριον ἔνθεν ἀκούω
> σιγαλέης λάλον εἷμα δυσηλακάτου Φιλομήλης,
> Τηρεὺς ἦν ἐμίαινεν, ὅτε ζυγίη φύγεν Ἥρη
> συζυγίην ἀχόρευτον ὀρεσσαύλων ὑμεναίων... [1]

---

[1] Ovid *Met.* VI 428–34; Nonnus *Dion.* IV 318–23. Musaeus (*Hero and Leander* 174 ff.) probably just copied Nonnus.

In both versions the absence of Juno Pronuba is observed, and the wedding-chorus is either not sung at all (in Nonnus) or provided by birds of ill omen (in Ovid).[1] Can this idea of doomed marriage or quasi-marriage come from the supposed Alexandrian original, whatever it was,[2] which Ovid and Nonnus used? It would be absurd to claim this as anything but a possibility; but if Catullus did mean to put his readers in mind of such an idea, they could connect poem 65 with one of the major themes of the long poems of Catullus.

The marriage-theme

Marriage, of course, is the subject of the *epithalamia* (Poems 61 and 62) and of one of the two narratives (Peleus and Thetis) in poem 64. But at a less obvious level it is also a theme which runs through all the long poems, with the exception of 63, and to which the reader's attention is drawn by the poet's careful repetition and cross-reference of words and images between one poem and another.[3]

In poem 64, for instance, it is not only the marriage-song of the Parcae which recalls the *epithalamia*,[4] but also the Ariadne episode, where at the mere narrative level the only relevance of weddings is Theseus' false promise to her.[5] The description of young Ariadne at the moment of falling in love with her "fair-haired guest" is composed almost entirely in imagery reminiscent of the wedding-

---

[1] Mr R. M. Ogilvie reminds me of *Aeneid* IV 166 ff., another ill-omened wedding witnessed by nature—but there Juno Pronuba "dat signum". Cf. also Ovid *Her.* II 115–20 (Phyllis and Demophoon).

[2] It is worth noting that Euphorion's *Thrax* dealt, among other stories, with that of Clymenus and Harpalyce (see Parthenius 13), which is closely parallel to the Procne/Tereus legend; and a surviving fragment of the poem (D. L. Page, *Greek Literary Papyri*, I (Loeb, London 1941), 494–9), dealing with Trambelus and Apriate, includes Apriate's curse that any future marriage of her murderer may be disastrous. Note also, as a parallel to the Ovid passage, Euphorion fr. 4P, from the *Apollodorus*, on birds of ill omen on Cyzicus' roof, forecasting the doom of his marriage to Larisa (Parthenius 28—incest, as in the Clymenus story).
Catullus' use of Euphorion (K. Latte, *Phil.* XC (1935), 154) depends entirely on the parallels of fr. 122P (possibly Neoptolemus, however) with 64.30, ἄταφος τάφος (Page, *op. cit.* 498) with 64.83 "funera nec funera", and the moralizing tone of the *Thrax* (*ibid.* 496) with that of 64.384–408. I am indebted to Mr Adrian Hollis for correspondence on this subject.

[3] On the marriage-theme in general, see Schäfer, pp. 73 ff., and P. McGushin, *CP* LXII (1967), 85 ff.

[4] e.g.: 64.329/61.19–20, 159 (good omens), 62.20 etc. (Hesperus); 64.331,335, 372/61.45 (*coniungere*); 64.374/61.56–8 (*dedere cupido marito*); 64.380/61.101 (*secubitus*).

[5] 64.141, 158.

songs—Ariadne too is in her mother's soft embrace, from which Theseus, like the bridegroom, will soon snatch her away, and her "chaste bed" is scented with the same flowers used to describe the bride in poem 61.[1] Similarly in poem 66, Callimachus' original referred to the same false tears shed by brides that Catullus observed in 62.36; but the most startling evidence for the continuity of the theme comes in lines 79–88, an address by Berenice's lock to new brides exhorting them to faithful love and *concordia*, which does not appear in the surviving papyrus of Callimachus' original poem.[2]

It is usually assumed that Callimachus himself added this passage later, when he included the *Coma* in his final edition of the *Aitia*; in our papyrus the poem forms part of a collection of "court poems", to which the supposed *aition* of the bride's libation in these lines would be irrelevant.[3] But if it is true that the whole poem "is as much an *aition* as the *Cydippe*, and has every right to be included in the *Aitia*",[4] it is not clear why any additional material should have been necessary for its inclusion. Moreover, it has been observed that the style and language of the lines are characteristically Catullan, and the possibility that they were inserted by Catullus himself should be seriously considered.[5] For here too the cross-references are very clear, not only to the *epithalamia*[6] but also to Ariadne: the "chaste bed" returns, and the bared breasts of line 81 recall not only those of the bride in 61, and those of Thetis when Peleus fell in love with her, but also those of Ariadne herself when first we meet her on the shore.[7]

The crux of this Catullan insertion in 66—if it is one—is the contrast between the *castum cubile* and the *impurus adulter* (lines

---

[1] 64.86 ff.; cf. 61.56–9 and 21–5, 62.21–3 and 39 ff. See F. Klingner, *Catulls Peleus-Epos* (Munich 1956), 82–3.

[2] E. Lobel, in *Oxyrhyncus Papyri*, XX (London 1952), 92, 98.

[3] R. Pfeiffer, *Callimachus*, II (Oxford 1953), xxxvii; C. M. Dawson, *YCS* XI (1950), 147.

[4] Dawson, *loc. cit.*

[5] M. C. J. Putnam, *CP* LV (1960), 223–8; cf. A. Salvatore, *Studi Catulliani* (Naples 1965), 278–84, esp. 278 n.22.

[6] 66.79/62.29, 66.80/61.45, etc., 66.81/62.60, 66.83/62.65, 66.84/61.58 and 98, 64.374, 66.88/61.227. If the lines *are* Callimachean, it must have been their relevance to his own obsessive themes that made Catullus translate the poem at all.

[7] 61.101, with the additional parallels of *deditus/dedit*, *adulter/adulterio* from 66.84; 64.16–18 (Thetis) and 64–66 (Ariadne). See Putnam, *loc. cit.* 226, 228 n. 15.

83–84, significantly placed in the middle).[1] The poem that follows is concerned entirely with adultery, and the seduction of the bride from Brixia;[2] but apart from this overt treatment of marriage and infidelity, which has its own epithalamic echoes,[3] Catullus' address to the house-door itself is in terms more appropriate to a bride. The first two lines could have come straight from a marriage-poem:[4]

> O dulci iucunda viro, iucunda parenti,
>   salve, teque bona Iuppiter auctet ope . . .

The joke lies in the unexpected *ianua* at the beginning of the third line, but the marriage idea is carried on four lines later, "postquam es porrecto *facta marita* sene".[5]

As for "poem 68", whether it is a *carmen* (lines 41–148) included in an epistolary frame, as is generally assumed nowadays,[6] or really two independent poems separated after line 40, as I prefer to think,[7] its first forty lines (68a) seem to introduce us, for the first time in the long poems, to Catullus' own love affairs, and in particular (apparently) to the unfaithfulness of his mistress in his absence.[8] This

[1] Putnam, *loc. cit.* 226.

[2] Also with (quasi) incest—see F. O. Copley, *TAPA* LXXX (1949), 251 on 67.19–28. Incest is also relevant to the situation of Berenice (66.22) and is used as an example of the degeneracy of the age at 64.401–4.

[3] 67.28/61.53, 67.36/61.97–8.

[4] 67.1–2; for the first line, cf. 62.58.

[5] 67.6 ("porrecto sene" double meaning?); cf. also 67.8–9—*fidem* and *tradita* appropriate to a bride (62.60, 66.81).

[6] Most recently Schäfer, p. 77.

[7] Despite the arguments of Professor Fraenkel (*Gn.* XXXIV (1962), 261–3), and A. Salvatore (*op. cit.* p. 21 n. 5 above, 97 ff.),I find the consistently different *ms* tradition for the proper names, at lines 12 and 30 on the one hand and 41, 50 and 150 on the other, more compelling than the supposed cross-references between lines 12 and 68 (the *hospitis officium* being the provision of a house for the lovers) and 32 and 149 ("I can't give you what you want . . . this is what I *can* do"). The last twelve lines of the poem, despite the different addressees, seem to me no less effective as a balance to lines 41–50—both on the survival of Allius' fame, with 149–52 picking up 41–4—than as a resumption of lines 1–40.

See Fordyce, pp. 342–3: Fraenkel effectively demolishes his second argument, but not (I think) his first and third on Lachmann's emendation *Mani* and the repeated brother-passage. On the other hand, it is true that the ending of 68a tails off rather unimpressively, but the poem's consistently loose and prosaic epistolary style may sufficiently account for this.

[8] 68.27–30, where Munro (pp. 172–3) may have been right to see a quotation in *oratio recta* from Mallius' letter. But the precise meaning of this passage is very uncertain.

is not, of course, the overt purpose of the poem, which is a *recusatio* to Mallius' request, but the effect of these lines (especially after the reference to Catullus' youthful affairs in lines 17–18) is to put the reader in mind of the poet's own mistress, just as the reason for the *recusatio* reminds him of the brother's death. Poem 68b, on the other hand, a fantastically careful construction of mingled myth and personal recollection,[1] is intimately concerned throughout with Catullus' mistress and the nature of his relationship with her.

The first of these two poems contains just one hint of the marriage-theme—the "*caelibe* lecto" on which the love-lorn Mallius tosses sleeplessly[2]—but in the second it is fundamental, and essential to our understanding of the poem. The first indication comes as soon as Catullus specifies what Allius' service to him was: "isque *domum* nobis isque dedit *dominae*", a collocation of nouns repeated at the end of the poem and reminiscent of the language of the first *epithalamium*.[3] He describes how his mistress came to him at Allius' house, "*coniugis* ut quondam . . ."; that is, not only does he compare her to the *bride* of Protesilaus, but underlines the comparison with the emphatic first word of the simile.[4] Laodamia gives way to Paris and Helen, the *adulterous* nature of whose love is mentioned at line 103; Paris and Helen to Hercules, whose *bride* (Hebe) is given as much space as his labours.[5] When the poet returns to himself and his mistress, she appears escorted by a Cupid wearing the same bridal *flammeum* as Hymen in poem 61.[6] He says he will put up with

---

[1] See J. Wohlberg, *CP* L (1955), 42–6 for the suggestion that the passage on the brother's death at 68.91–100 was inserted after the composition of the Laodamia-simile, the symmetrical structure of which it interrupts. However, I would divide the original structure more simply than Wohlberg does, into four twelve-line sections: 73–84 on Laodamia and Protesilaus, 85–90/101–7 (*coniugium*) on Helen and Paris, 107–18 on Hercules, 119–30 on Laodamia-similes. On either side of this structure we have 41–50 and 149–60 on Allius (see p. 22 n. 7 above), 51–72 and 131–48 on Catullus and Lesbia. The *omphalos* of the whole design would then be *coniugium* in line 107, and the end of the second half (160) would match the end of the first (106 *vita dulcius*).

[2] 68.6, cf. 6.6 "viduas noctes" and 66.22 "orbum cubile".

[3] 68.68,156; 61.31. For the symbolic importance of the idea of the *domus* in Catullus, see M. C. J. Putnam, *CP* LVII (1962), 13, and especially Schäfer, pp. 75–6, 85, 88–9.

[4] 68.73; also 81 *coniugis*, 84 *coniugio*, 107 *coniugium*. Cf. Schäfer, pp. 80 ff, and P. McGushin, *CP* LXII (1967), 87–8.

[5] Note the reference to her virginity in 116 (cf. 61.4, 20, etc.) and the *iugum ferre* of 119 (cf. 64.302, 68.81, both bridal contexts).

[6] 68.133–4; on this passage, see the excellent treatment of Sheridan Baker, *CP* LV (1960), 171–3, esp. 172.

C

her *rara furta* as Juno did with the infidelities of Jupiter—a remark-
ably ambiguous passage which indicates both the quasi-marital
possessiveness of the poet's passion and his consciousness that it was
itself adulterous; both points are made explicit in the following lines,
where he admits that his mistress came to him not like a bride on
her father's arm, but furtively at night, and from her husband's
gremium, not her mother's.[1]

Clearly weddings and marriage-imagery meant a lot to Catullus,
and were deeply relevant to his conception of his own love-affair.[2]
It is thus not entirely far-fetched to suppose that this recurring
theme is the main criterion of arrangement for the long poems,
along with the metrical division at (and announced by) poem 65.
The ideas set out in the *epithalamia* are developed through the
ambiguous auguries of the Parcae in 64,[3] the plea for fidelity in 66
and the unfaithful reality of 67, into the quasi-marital celebration
in 68b of the poet's own love, adulterous and doomed.[4]

Such a hypothesis would explain the apparent anomaly at 65.14
as a reminder, like *caelibe* in 68a, that the theme should still be kept
in mind. We might also account for the ten-line insertion into the
Callimachus translation if it were not part of Catullus' original
version, but inserted when he was arranging the long poems in
order to bring out the continuity of the marriage theme.[5] But
as in the 1–60 collection, Catullus must have found that not all the

---

[1] 68.136 ff, 143–6; compare 61.57–9, 62.21–2 and *gremium* at 68.132, where "*se
contulit*" (like "*se* intulit" at 70–1) may be intended to contrast with an escorted
bride.

[2] Particularly if the first version of 68b, his most ambitious attempt to distil the
affair into poetry, was centred on the word *coniugium* (p. 23 n. 1 above). Cf. Fraenkel,
pp. 417, 419 on "the manner in which Horace sometimes places in the centre of the
poem a thought whose significance he wishes to accentuate".

[3] See Klingner, *op. cit.* (p. 21 n. 1 above) 23: Catullus alone has the *Fates* singing the
wedding-song (cf. p. 20 above on his possible reference to equally sinister choristers
in the Procne story); Apollo, who with the Muses fulfils this duty in the usual version
of the legend, is kept out of the way (64.299). The ironical *quare* of line 372 points in
the same direction: "Polyxena is going to be killed—so on with the wedding!"

[4] See Ferrero, pp. 93 and 146f on the apprehension implicit in the Laodamia simile,
and Baker, *loc. cit.* 172 on the bad omen of 68.71–2 (contrast 61.159–60).

[5] This might count as a parallel for Wohlberg's hypothesis of the subsequent insertion of 68.91–100 (p. 23 n. 1 above), if Catullus, arranging the long poems, felt that the
stress laid on the brother's death required more subsequent justification than the
passage in 68a, and therefore wrote in a further lament at the only other appropriate
place—the reference to Troy in 68b.

poems he wished to publish admitted of arrangement or easy amendment to fit his scheme: in the long poems, the *Attis* (63) is clearly not immediately relevant, but placed by more formal criteria, to separate the two poems in hexameters and lead up to the longer work in the same *genre*, poem 64.[1]

The epigrams

In view of this marriage-theme in 61–8, it may be significant that poem 70, the first of the Lesbia-poems in the collection of short elegiac pieces (69–116) begins: "nulli se dicit mulier mea *nubere* malle . . .".[2] However, the idea is not followed up in subsequent poems, and the criterion of arrangement for the epigram-collection itself must be sought elsewhere.

With no opportunity for metrical variation, the only criterion here is subject-matter. At the very start there is an alternation of theme,[3] with 69/71 on the man with the armpits, 70/72 on Lesbia and Jupiter. This pattern is not continued, but there is close interconnection of language and subject in 70–72–75 and 73–76–77–87, as well as in the Gellius poems (74, 80, 88–91, 116?). In this series, the poems on Lesbia are not arranged to illustrate the development of the affair; with the exception of 86, which I would class as an occasional poem in which Lesbia's presence is secondary,[4] they are all variations on the static themes of Lesbia's infidelity, Catullus' attempts to come to terms with his simultaneous disillusionment and desire,[5] and the disloyalty both of her and of his friends in contrast with his own *pietas*.

Most of the poems which separate those on Lesbia are lampoons of one sort or another, so the analysis of this collection has to be taken further than that of 1–60. In Table II I have subdivided the lampoons by isolating two obsessively recurring themes, incest and *irrumatio* (INC, IRR); the other categories are as used in Table I.

---

[1] So G. Lieberg, *RFIC* XXXVI (1958), 30.

[2] Not necessarily meant literally, of course: compare *tenere* in the parallel passage 72.2, and Plaut. *Cist.* 43 f., *Cas.* 486.

[3] Like 2(2a)3, 5(6)7, 16(17)21(22)23, 37(38)39 and perhaps 41(42)43 in the 1–60 collection.

[4] Compare poems 36–40 (p. 15 above).

[5] See S. Commager, *HSCP* LXX (1965), 93 ff., and F. O. Copley, *AJP* LXX (1949), 24–33 on the attempt at "self-information" in these poems. However, there is a significant development in the first two (parallel) Lesbia-poems, 70 and 72.

TABLE II

69.	Noli admirari quare tibi femina nulla		I	
70.	Nulli se dicit mulier mea nubere malle	L		
71.	Siquoi iure bono sacer alarum obstitit hircus		I	
72.	Dicebas quondam solum te nosse Catullum	L		
73.	Desine de quoquam quicquam bene velle mereri			
74.	Gellius audierat patruum obiurgare solere			INC IRR
75.	Huc est mens deducta tua, mea Lesbia, culpa	L		
76.	Siqua recordanti benefacta priora voluptas	L		
77.	Rufe, mihi frustra ac nequiquam credite amice	(L)		
78.	Gallus habet fratres, quorum est lepidissima coniunx			INC
78a.	(Sed nunc id doleo, quod purae pura puellae)			IRR
79.	Lesbius est pulcher; quid ni? quem Lesbia malit	L		INC IRR
80.	Quid dicam, Gelli, quare rosea ista labella			IRR
81.	Nemone in tanto potuit populo esse, Iuventi	J		
82.	Quinti, si tibi vis oculos debere Catullum	L?		
83.	Lesbia mi praesente viro mala plurima dicit	L		
84.	Chommoda dicebat, si quando commoda vellet			
85.	Odi et amo, quare id faciam fortasse requiris	L		
86.	Quintia formosa est multis; mihi candida, longa	(L)		
87.	Nulla potest mulier tantum se dicere amatam	L		
88.	Quid facit is, Gelli, qui cum matre atque sorore			INC IRR
89.	Gellius est tenuis; quid ni? cui tam bona mater			INC
90.	Nascatur magus ex Gelli matrisque nefando			INC
91.	Non ideo, Gelli, sperabam te mihi fidum	(L)		INC
92.	Lesbia mi dicit semper male nec tacet umquam	L		
93.	Nil nimium studeo, Caesar, tibi velle placere		(I)	
94.	Mentula moechatur; moechatur mentula certe		I	
95.	Zmyrna mei Cinnae nonam post denique messem			
96.	Si quicquam mutis gratum acceptumve sepulcris			
97.	Non (ita me di ament) quicquam referre putavi		I	
98.	In te, si in quemquam, dici pote, putide Victi		I	
99.	Surripui tibi, dum ludis, mellite Iuventi	J		
100.	Caelius Aufillenum et Quintius Aufillenam	(L)		
101.	Multas per gentes et multa per aequora vectus			
102.	Si quicquam tacito commissum est fido ab amico			
103.	Aut sodes mihi redde decem sestertia, Silo		(I)	
104.	Credis me potuisse meae maledicere vitae	(L)	(I)	
105.	Mentula conatur Pipleium scandere montem		I	
106.	Cum puero bello praeconem qui vidit esse		(I)	
107.	Si quidquam cupido optantique obtigit umquam	L		

108.	Si, Comini, populi arbitrio tua cana senectus	I	
109.	Iucundum, mea vita, mihi proponis amorem	L	
110.	Aufillena, bonae semper laudantur amicae		
111.	Aufillena, viro contentam vivere solo		INC
112.	Multus homo es, Naso, neque tecum multus homost qui	I	
113.	Consule Pompeio primum duo, Cinna, solebant	(I)	
114.	Firmanus saltus non falso, Mentula, dives	I	
115.	Mentula habet instar triginta iugera prati	I	
116.	Saepe tibi studioso animo venante requirens		

Another recurring idea, that of "facinus facere",[1] should be noticed as linking the sin of Lesbia's betrayal with those of the other victims of Catullus' anger. Even though the categories are less obvious than in 1–60, and less easily distinguishable, it is clear that the elegiac collection falls into two halves separated at 92–3. The incest and *irrumatio* themes so frequent in 69–92 appear only once in the second half,[2] which (on the other hand) contains almost all the occasional verse not linked to Lesbia and her lovers. All the Mentula-poems appear in the second half, all those on Gellius, except 116, in the first.[3]

It is noticeable that poem 116 contains two metrical features unique in Catullus: the entirely spondaic third line and the elided *s* in line 8. One at least of these was considered old-fashioned in Catullus' time,[4] and it is tempting to suppose that the poem is a spurious addition, attached after the publication of the collection; Catullus may indeed have written it, but not wanted to include so *illepidus* a piece of versification in his published works. If this were indeed the case, then the distinction between the two halves would be even more conspicuous.

The first half, 69–92, contains a high proportion of interrelating poems, and very few which relate to epigrams in the second half.[5]

---

[1] 75.4, 81.6, 88?, 91.10?, 104.4, 110.4.

[2] 111.4 (incest). See Ferrero, p. 280 on the development of the Aufillena poems: in 100 she is Quintius' girl-friend, with no hint of disapproval, but in 110 she is an expensive mistress no better than a prostitute, and in 111 she has sunk to the incestuous level of Gellius and Lesbius.

[3] See Barwick, pp. 316–17 for these cycles.

[4] Cic. *orator* 161; Quinn, p. 46. It is conceivable, however, that 116.8 may be a deliberately calculated effect, like the repeated elisions of 73.6.

[5] 82/92 with 104? 76/87 with 107/109? 78a.2 with 99.10?

It is not only homogeneous but coherently organized. The reader is introduced first to Rufus and then to Lesbia's infidelity in the alternating first four poems of the sequence; the two are connected at poem 77, where it appears that Rufus is guilty of an affair with Lesbia—and where the reader realizes in retrospect that Rufus must be the faithless friend of poem 73. In exactly the same way Gellius is introduced, and the list of his vices gone through in increasingly disapproving terms,[1] before it is revealed in poem 91 that he too was a lover of Lesbia.[2] In the middle of the Gellius-cycle, and placed between two poems which illustrate to the reader the point of the last line,[3] is poem 79 on Lesbius, which unites the recurring ideas of incest and *irrumatio* with the theme of Lesbia's other lovers. So these interlocking sequences on the other men in Lesbia's life provide a counterpoint to the main theme of Catullus' own attitude to her.

If it is accepted that 69–92 is a cycle complete in itself—though relieved with occasional poems on other subjects, such as 81 and 84—then perhaps 93 on Caesar will count as the programme poem which announces the change in theme. The first poem of the Mentula cycle comes immediately after it—and Mentula, whether Mamurra or not,[4] was surely a partisan of Caesar enriched from Gaul in the way Mamurra was. Besides, of the other men named in the poems after no. 93, Cominius (108) may reasonably be identified as the Caesarian Q. Cominius who appears with L. Ticida—presumably the poet—in 48 B.C.;[5] Silo (103) was surely a Marsic Poppaedius, "saevus et indomitus" as befitted a man with a proud heritage among the unconquerable Marsi, and therefore perhaps identical with the Caesarian senator of that name;[6] and Tappo (104.4) is a characteristically Cisalpine *cognomen*,[7] known at Rome

---

[1] Schäfer, pp. 30–1; cf. p. 27 n. 2 above (Aufillena).

[2] Barwick, p. 317: 91 put last in the cycle as representing the crux of Catullus' attack.

[3] 78a.2/79.4/80.8. The "pura puella" of 78a might even be Lesbia herself.

[4] Barwick (*loc. cit.*) considers the identification certain because of 29.13. Tenney Frank's theory that he was Labienus (*AJP* XL (1919) 407–8) is not compelling: 114.1 need not refer to Mentula's home town.

[5] *Bell. Afr.* 44, 46. Alternatively, cf. *CQ* XV (1965), 159–60 for a possibly Caesarian senator from Narbo, (Co)minius Longinus (*ILLRP* 296).

[6] Dio XLVIII 41.1; R. Syme, *Roman Revolution* (Oxford 1939), 91. Cf. Appian *BC* I 46 *ad fin.* on the Marsi.

[7] *CIL* V index; known only twice outside Cisalpina (*CIL* XI 7127, XIV 3945). There were, however, senatorial Valerii Tappones in the early second century (*pr.* 192, *tr. pl.* 188).

from the Aquileian senator C. Appuleius Tappo,[1] who was probably one of Caesar's Gallic senators and might well have been among his hopeful followers in the fifties. If all the men attacked in this part of the collection were Caesarians,[2] then 93–116 would have a certain homogeneity and poem 93 itself would be an appropriate introduction.

As with the later stages of the 1–60 collection, this second main group of epigrams is much more loosely organized than the first. It is more liberally interspersed with occasional poems and unconnected squibs, and the criteria for the juxtaposition of poems, where they can be guessed, are much more haphazard: for instance, 101 may come after 100 because of "fraternum dulce sodalicium", and 97 and 98 may belong together because of "culum lingere".[3] But if 116 is really spurious, then Catullus finished this group as he began it, with Mentula,[4] and completed his collection on a line any lampoonist would be glad to leave in his reader's mind: "non homo, sed vero mentula magna minax".

How many books?

Each of the three main divisions of the collection as we have it (1–60; 61–8; 69–115/116) thus shows an internally coherent and consistent arrangement which can hardly be the work of anyone but the poet himself. Can we then postulate three *libelli*, joined at some later stage to form the book, large by ancient standards,[5] that has come down to us? In that case, 1–60 might be the book known to Martial as the "Passer Catulli", and 69 ff. possibly a book of epigrams like that of Callimachus.[6] However, the three parts would

---

[1] *ILLRP* 436, cf. 540, *CIL* I² 2205.

[2] Aemilius and Victius (97, 98) are unidentifiable; Naso (112) might be P. Naso, pr. 44, and/or the Sextius Naso among the tyrannicides (Cic. *Phil.* III 25, App. *BC* II 113). Cf. also R. Syme, *Hist.* VIII (1959), 211 on Victor (80.7)—perhaps a friend of Antony (Cic. *Att.* XIV 14.2).

[3] 100.4; 97.11, 98.4.

[4] Cf. p. 14 above on poems 28 and 47 (Piso) opening and closing a homogeneous sequence.

[5] Wheeler, pp. 14–17; F. G. Kenyon, *Books and Readers in Ancient Greece and Rome* (2nd ed., Oxford 1951), 54 ff. on the length of extant papyrus rolls; T. Birt, *Das Antike Buchwesen* (Berlin 1882), 289 ff.

[6] Martial IV 14 (cf. Wheeler, pp. 19 f.). Testimonia to Callimachus' *epigrammata* in R. Pfeiffer, *Callimachus* I (Oxford 1949), 323–7.

be very unequal in length—respectively 842, 1123 and 319 lines.[1] Besides, the ancient citations of Catullus show no indication of separate books, numbered or not; the references seem to be to individual poems.[2]

There are also certain connections between the three groups which might suggest that the poet did not publish them separately. The most noticeable of these are between poem 68(b) and certain of the epigrams: not only does the long elegy explore the nature of Catullus' love affair in a way similar to the shorter elegiac poems on Lesbia, but the *nubere* of 70.2 and several other verbal similarities look like explicit cross-references to poem 68.[3] These might just indicate that the poems were *written* at the same time, when Catullus had these ideas in mind, without any implications about arrangement or publication; but it would be a curious coincidence if the elegiac short poems in our collection followed the longer poems in the same metre purely fortuitously, after the announcement of the change of metre at 65.12. There are also certain very noticeable parallel passages which connect the long poems with the 1–60 collection—notably the stars-and-sand simile in 61 and Scylla and the lioness in 64[4]—and it is highly probable that the reader's recognition of Mentula in the epigrams is meant to depend on his knowledge of poem 29.[5] Do these indications mean that the whole book as it stands was published at once, or that the three main parts were published in their present order but successively, with the poet assuming that his readers would recognize allusions to the earlier collections? The absence of references to numbered books still seems to rule out the second alternative.

Wilamowitz considered it irrelevant whether the poems were sold in one roll, or in one *capsula* containing three rolls,[6] but the rolls would surely need to be numbered if it was necessary for them to

---

[1] Wheeler (p. 18) makes a division after 64, with the result that the parts would be 842, 797 and 645 lines long.

[2] O. Weinreich, *Her.* LXXXVII (1959), 88 n. 3.

[3] e.g. 107.6/68.148 (*candidiore nota*), 77.4/68.158 (*omnia nostra bona*), 101.5/64.218, 101.6/68.20 and 92; cf. also 78b.4/68.46, 76.18/68.4?

[4] 61.199 ff./7.2–8, 64.154 ff./60.1–3; cf. also 61.53,160/2a.2–3, and Schäfer, pp. 43–4, 77 on 64.133 ff. (etc.)/30 and 61.46 f./45.20.

[5] Schäfer (p. 26) would add 81.2 and 26.4, but "bellus homo" in the former passage is more likely to remind the reader of 78.3.

[6] *Op. cit.* (p. 1 n. 4 above) 292 n. 3.

be read in order. Could the entire work have formed one roll? At this comparatively early stage of the Roman book-trade, perhaps a *liber* of over 2300 lines was not out of the question.[1] In that case poem 1, with its diminutive "libellus" and self-deprecating "nugae", would have to be introductory to a *large* book, and one which contained the poet's most ambitious work. This is not inconceivable: the *libellus* sent by Calvus at the Saturnalia cannot have been a *little* book, particularly if the contributors were as profuse as Suffenus or Hortensius,[2] and the *nugae* of which Nepos had approved might be identified with the poems of the first part only (1–60). Each solution has its difficulties. The "single roll" theory presupposes a departure by Catullus from Callimachus' famous maxim; the "three rolls" theory fails to explain the absence of numbered books. Perhaps the problem had better be left unsettled.

The possibility cannot be ruled out that some of the poems had already been grouped and published in smaller collections, for one of which poem 1 was originally written. But there is no real evidence for any stage in publication between the first circulation of poems—presumably in *pugillaria* or *codicilli* among the poet's circle of acquaintances (42, 50.2)—and the final collection.[3] All the indications are that our collection, with the possible exception of 116, is the *liber Catulli* (or the three component parts of it), as arranged and published by the poet himself.

---

[1] Wilamowitz' solution (*loc. cit.*); compare Lucretius' fifth book (1457 lines) and Apollonius Rhodius' fourth (1799). See Birt, *op. cit.* (p. 29 n. 5 above) 291–3, though he observes (p. 293) that Catullus and his friends might be expected to have favoured shorter books.

[2] 14.12; cf. lines 5–7 "*tot* poetis . . . *tantum* impiorum", 22.3–4, 95.3.

[3] Cf. Hor. *Ep.* I 20.1–5 (esp. 4 "paucis ostendi") for the two stages.

PART TWO

IV

CHRONOLOGICAL CONSEQUENCES

THIS conclusion, if it is valid, illustrates the way Catullus worked, and the way (like Callimachus) he distinguished various parts of his poetry; in particular, it invalidates Wheeler's contention that "Catullus regarded his little elegiac poems as not essentially different from the little poems in hendecasyllables and choliambics".[1] It rids us of the idea that Catullus died pen in hand, as it were, without having time to arrange his poems for publication, an assumption that has led scholars to give more credence than they perhaps deserve to Jerome's data on the poet's age at death.[2] But there are other more unexpected consequences.

Poem 51

Poem 51 has been traditionally regarded by English-speaking critics as one of the first poems Catullus wrote to Lesbia, if not the very first of all—a supposition which requires the last stanza to be detached and treated as a fragment of a different poem in Sapphics of which nothing else survives. Thus Landor declared in 1842 that "the ode ends, and always ended, with *lumina nocte*", and Davies in 1876 called it "a happy and shrewd instinct which places first in the series that model translation from Sappho's Greek fragment which seems at once a naming-day ode and a declaration of passion"; Fordyce (1961) assents to both these views, though expressing them with a more scholarly caution.[3] This tradition has been challenged

---

[1] Wheeler, ch. 2, esp. pp. 38 ff. (quotation from p. 47). *Contra* Schäfer, pp. 58–9, Commager *loc. cit.* (p. 2 n. 3 above), 98–9, 105, and J. P. Elder, *HSCP* LX (1951), 111–12.

[2] Though we do know from Ovid (*am.* III 9.61) that he died young.

[3] *The Works of Walter Savage Landor* (ed. T. E. Welby, London 1930), vol. IX p. 208; the Rev. J. Davies, *Catullus, Tibullus and Propertius* (Edinburgh 1876), 18; Fordyce, pp. 218–19.

by D. A. Kidd, who treats the fourth stanza as an integral part of the whole; its theme of destruction is anticipated by the physical symptoms of the second and third stanzas, which are made more intense than Sappho's original and which Kidd sees as analogous to the "foul disease" from which Catullus asks release in poem 76. But despite his penetrating analysis, tradition dies hard: an even more recent critic still sees 51 as illustrating "wonder and joy and an almost maidenly shyness coupled with reverential awe" for Lesbia.[1]

If Catullus himself arranged the poems, then we can say firmly that Kidd is right and the older tradition wrong. Firstly, it is surely inconceivable that Catullus would have abandoned metrical *variatio* to the point of putting two Sapphic poems together, no. 11 being the only other one in the entire collection; the fourth stanza must belong to poem 51, and we must interpret all four as a whole. Secondly and more important, since the poem is placed outside (and after) the Lesbia-cycle in the first group of poems, the reader knows the story of the affair and is not baffled by the sombre apprehensiveness of the last stanza. He is also expected to know Sappho's original, and will see that most of the details Catullus himself has added—"identidem", "misero . . . mihi", and the emphatic "nocte" at the end of the third stanza—are echoes of the Lesbia-cycle itself, and in particular the bitter last stages of it.[2] The Sapphic metre and the *identidem* repeated at the same point in the stanza have often been cited as evidence for deliberate cross-reference between poems 11 and 51, in the belief that 51 is the first Lesbia-poem and 11 the last, bitterly recalling the innocent outset of the affair.[3] But it is now clear that 51 was not composed in the first flush of love, and whichever poem was actually written first, the poet's own arrangement makes 51 refer back to 11, and not *vice versa*.

---

[1] D. A. Kidd, *Aumla* XX (1963), 298–308, esp. 304 ff.; P. McGushin, *CP* LXII (1967), 87, etc. E. A. Fredricksmeyer, *TAPA* XCVI, (1965), 153–64, is in substantial agreement with Kidd, though evidently unaware of his article.

[2] 51.3/11.19, 51.4–5/8.1, 51.12/5.6. *Eripit* (51.6) is another Catullan touch: cf. 76.20, 77.4–5, etc.

[3] E.g. J. W. Mackail, *Latin Literature* (London 1895), 57 n.; R. Y. Tyrrell, *Latin Poetry* (London 1895), 105–6; Tenney Frank, *Catullus and Horace* (New York 1928), 19, 92. Tyrrell (*op. cit.* 91) bases his rejection of the order of the poems in our collection on the priority of poem 51: "editors [*sic*] continue to present us in the eleventh ode with the final repudiation of Lesbia, while we have in the fifty-first the rapture of reciprocated love".

So the conclusion that Catullus arranged his own poems as we have them requires a modification of the "internal" history of the Lesbia affair. It also helps us with the external evidence about certain historical questions, which are discussed below.

The quarrel with Caesar and the brother's death

Since the collection as arranged and published by Catullus contains poems 29 and 57, either it was published before the reconciliation with Caesar recorded by Suetonius (*DJ* 73), or else that reconciliation did not represent a whole-hearted conversion. (The offending poems had, of course, already been circulated, but Catullus could have kept them out of his collection if he had wanted to.) The inclusion of poem 11 would seem to require that some sort of reconciliation had taken place, unless the compliment of "Caesaris . . . monimenta magni" is insincere. Moreover, it may well be, as Ferrero suggests, that the Mentula-poems (if they are indeed about Mamurra) only employ the pseudonym because of Caesar's objection to the attacks on Mamurra by name.[1] Our interpretation of poem 93 may bear this out; an occasional poem should contain within it the information necessary for its comprehension, and the reader might well infer from poem 93 that Catullus *should* "want to please" Caesar. That is, it makes more sense if written *after* the interview when Caesar complained of the lampoons against himself and Mamurra. The poet is then saying: "you want me to please you, Caesar, but I shan't do that; nor shall I attack you, for I am quite indifferent". But he goes on to attack Caesar's friends instead, including Mamurra again, though not by name.

It is thus probable that the "reconciliation" with Caesar did not mean very much. Catullus may have promised not to attack Caesar (and Mamurra) again directly, but he did not feel obliged to omit the poems at which Caesar originally took offence from his published collection, nor did the agreement extend to Caesar's less influential friends. Cicero's palinode after Luca may be a parallel case, since his new *amicitia* did not prevent him from attacking Caesar's father-in-law, L. Piso. Aemilius, Victius and the rest were much smaller fry than Piso, of course, but Catullus was much less dangerous as a potential opponent than Cicero.

[1] Ferrero, p. 70. Suet. *DJ* 73: "sibi versiculis de Mamurra perpetua stigmata imposita non dissimulaverat".

When was the agreement made? The internal evidence of the poems (29 on Britain) allows any date after late 55 B.C. Caesar was available for diplomatic dinner-parties in Verona during the winters of 55/4, 54/3 and 53/2 B.C.[1] If Catullus made his peace with Caesar at the same time as his ex-proconsul Memmius,[2] then the first of these winters must be assumed. In any case, the most natural hypothesis is to put it as near as possible to the years 56–54 B.C., to which all the dateable poems of Catullus are to be assigned.[3]

The meeting with Caesar took place in Verona, as Suetonius' reference to Catullus' father implies; it must in any case have been somewhere in Caesar's province. It was presumably also in Verona that the poet carried on his feud with Mamurra (cf. 43.5–6); we must remember that the province of Cisalpine Gaul was a popular place with Roman high society when Caesar and his staff were wintering there.[4] Lesbia herself was certainly not unknown to the *provincia* that called Mamurra's mistress beautiful (43.6–7): poem 86 compares her with a Quintia who was certainly Veronese, and Quintia's brother was evidently paying some attention to her. Their fellow-townsman Caelius was a true friend to Catullus "cum vesana meas torreret flamma medullas"—surely a reference to his affair with Lesbia.[5]

No doubt Catullus went to Verona every winter. Poem 14 sees him at Rome for the Saturnalia, but if the Valerii of Verona kept the old Roman festivals, we should expect a man to whom the home and the family were important (as they certainly were to Catullus) to be at home on February 22nd, the traditional day of family reunion following the Parentalia.[6] But in any case, it is quite illegitimate to assume that his stay there after returning from Bithynia (poem 31) must be the same as his stay after his brother's

[1] Not 52/1—see Hirt. *BG* VIII 4.

[2] As assumed in *JRS* LVI (1966), 113 n. 65. Memmius had Caesar's support for his consular candidature by July 54 at least (Cic. *Att.* IV 15.7).

[3] See p. 47 below.

[4] Plut. *Caes.* 20.3 (cf. 21 on the throng of senators at Luca in 56). E.g.: P. Sestius, Nov. 58 (Cic. *Sest.* 71); Ap. Claudius and M. Crassus, spring 56 (*QF* II 4.6, *Fam.* I 9.9); Cicero, late in 53 (*Att.* VIII 1.4, Ravenna).

[5] 82 (Quintius), 100.1–2.

[6] Ovid *Fasti* II 617 ff., Val. Max. II 1.8; A. Degrassi, *Inscriptiones Italiae* XIII (Rome 1947), 2.414. See p. 23 n. 3 above.

death (68a). There is no evidence for the traditional hypothesis that Catullus visited his brother's tomb while on his Bithynian journey.[1]

The few references to the death of Catullus' brother would seem to indicate a comparatively late date for this event, if it was really the devastating loss the poet tells us it was.[2] He does not link it with the poems about his sojourn with Memmius; indeed, the two subjects are carefully separated. When, if at all, he made the journey to the tomb implied in 101, we shall never know. It is quite possible that the journey belongs only to "the world of the poems"; though the reader is to imagine the poet at the tomb, this is a necessary element in the type of poem Catullus chose to write, and cannot be pressed as autobiography. It is true that the first line, which mentions a voyage, is not paralleled in the other known poem of the genre,[3] but Catullus wanted to say not only that his brother was dead and that he loved him, but also that he died far away. (On a different level the Priapean fragment 1 may be analogous, since we need hardly assume that Catullus *really* dedicated a grove to Priapus on the Hellespontine coast.)

But whether Catullus went to the tomb or not, the only possible *terminus ante quem* for his brother's death before the unknown date of the compilation of the collection itself is that inferred from the apparent reference to an interruption in poetic output at 68.15–20.[4] How long this lasted it is impossible to say;[5] the poetry Catullus then

[1] See Maas, p. 79.

[2] This is particularly true if the "brother-passage" in 68b was a later insertion (p. 23 n. 1 above).
The dating of 68b relies on the hypothetical identification of Lesbia with Clodia Metelli (on which see ch. VI below), and on such attempts to detect the "internal" history of the affair as led Ellis (p. 131) to put 68.135 ff. well before poem 37, and Maas (p. 82) to put it after. 68b and 37 are very different types of poem, and no doubt the poet's state of mind was very different when he wrote each of them; but that does not make it impossible that they are contemporary, nor that they refer to the same lovers of Lesbia. All we can safely say is that lines 135 ff. of 68b were not written in the first flush of Catullus' infatuation.

[3] Meleager, *Anth. Pal.* VII 476. (Note the similarity of 101.1 to Theocritus 17.77.)

[4] Even this depends on the view (Munro, p. 171 f.) that *lusi* and *studium* (cf. *studia* 68.26) refer to love poetry, which was strongly denied by Ellis (p. 405 f.) and Kroll (p. 222)—perhaps rightly.

[5] The view of poem 65 taken above (p. 18) does not, of course, mean that Catullus had not previously written the elegiac poems, but merely that he used it as a convenient introduction to them in the collection.

abandoned ("multa satis lusi") may have been practically identical with the whole of the collection as we have it.

Veranius and Fabullus

What Catullus links with his Bithynian adventure is not his brother's death but the unprofitable journey of his friends Veranius and Fabullus to Spain. It is generally assumed nowadays that the pair made two journeys, first to Spain under an unknown proconsul, then to Macedonia in 57 B.C. under L. Piso Caesoninus.[1] But if Catullus arranged the poems himself, it is very hard to believe this: the parallelism of his own return from Bithynia and Veranius' from Spain (poems 9–13) and of his attacks on Memmius and on Piso (28–47) make it clear that there was only one journey—to Spain under a Piso.[2] When did it take place?

Poems 28 and 47 were evidently written by Catullus at Rome while his friends were still away,[3] and perhaps we are also to infer from 12.13–15 that Veranius and Fabullus were still absent when this poem was written. In poem 12 Catullus is at Rome, and so, evidently, is young C. Asinius Pollio. A man called Pollio left Rome in February or March of 56 B.C. to visit P. Lentulus Spinther in Cilicia; he was a political supporter of Spinther, and since Asinius Pollio's first prosecution was against Spinther's inimicus C. Cato, it is reasonable to identify the two. There is an objection: Cinna wrote Asinius Pollio's propempticon, and should therefore have been in Rome in the spring of 56 B.C., but he is generally considered to have been in Bithynia with Catullus at this very time.[4] However, this difficulty is illusory, since the article devoted to Parthenius in the Suda mentions Cinna in Bithynia about 66 or 65 B.C., and that must have been the time when he picked up the eight sturdy litter-bearers of whom Catullus too rashly claimed ownership.[5] So Cinna had not gone with Catullus to Bithynia; the man who left for

---

[1] So R. Syme, CM XVII (1956), 129–34; R. G. M. Nisbet, Cicero in L. Calpurnium Pisonem oratio (Oxford 1961), 180–2; Fordyce, p. 113.

[2] As assumed without argument by Barwick (p. 316); it is, of course, a corollary of the idea of a cycle of poems. Cf. also Maas, p. 80.

[3] Nisbet, op. cit. 181–2.

[4] Cic. Fam. I 6.1; Att. IV 15.4, 16.5, Tac. dial. 34 (C. Cato prosecution); R. Syme, JRS LI (1961), 23–4.

[5] 10.18–32; A. Rostagni, AAT LXVIII (1932–3), 502–13, esp. 508–11.

Cilicia in the spring of 56 B.C. was Asinius Pollio; and poem 12 can hardly have been written between the spring of 57 (Catullus' departure for Bithynia) and whenever Pollio returned.

Probably Pollio was not away long: Spinther needed his friends in Rome to help arrange the Egyptian command for him—the question of who should have it was still open until Gabinius invaded Egypt in the spring of 55 B.C. Possibly then Pollio came back in the autumn of 56, presumably not long after Catullus returned from his tour of the "famous cities of Asia"; and at that time Veranius and Fabullus were still away. They had been away longer than expected,[1] so 56 was clearly not their first year of absence; no doubt they too had followed a magistrate of 58 B.C. to his province in the spring of 57.

But which magistrate? Except for the province, Piso Caesoninus would be the obvious candidate, though some of the arguments advanced in support of the identification are merely specious:[2] Piso's Epicureanism and patronage of poets are irrelevant to Veranius and Fabullus, who (so far as we know) were neither poets nor Epicureans; the phrase *frigora et fames*, used both by Catullus and by Cicero in the *in Pisonem*, is a commonplace which cannot be pressed for identifying the provinces concerned;[3] Greeks like Socration might appear in a cultivated Roman's entourage in any province;[4] and any Piso, not just Caesoninus, would qualify as a *nobilis amicus* (28.13). But is there another Piso available in 58 B.C.?

Cicero's son-in-law C. Piso Frugi, quaestor in 58 B.C., was *Luci filius*; this should imply an elder brother L. Piso—who might well have been a praetor in that year. An elder son of L. Piso Frugi, *pr.* 74, holding the same office as his father only sixteen years later, seems at first sight unlikely; but the praetor of 74 B.C., himself son of a praetor of *c.* 112 and grandson of a praetor of 138, evidently reached the office comparatively late in life, and a son in the same

---

[1] 28.4 ("satisne . . . tulistis?"); 28.2 suggests that they have just travelled back.

[2] Ellis, pp. 91–2; Nisbet, *op. cit.* 181.

[3] 28.5, Cic. *Pis.* 40. See *TLL* VI 232 for the frequent collocation of *fames* with *frigus* (less often with *algus*).

[4] *SEG* XV 254 for Greeks in Gaul under Cn. Ahenobarbus, *cos.* 122 B.C. Note also Polybius in Spain (Pol. III 59.7), Posidonius in Spain and Gaul (Strabo III 144, 172, IV 198), and later Xenophon of Cos in Britain (*SIG* I² 368). Cn. Pompeius Magni l. Lenaeus was "paene omnium expeditionum comes" with his patron (Suet. *gramm.* 15), which might imply a trip to Spain.

D

magistracy in 58 B.C. would give a very reasonable average gap of 27 years over three generations.[1] The detection of a Piso who could have been praetor in 58 B.C. and thereafter proconsul of Hither Spain is thus not impossible, and the creation of a second journey (to Macedonia) for Veranius and Fabullus becomes unnecessary.

Volusius

Poems 28 on Piso, 29 on Mamurra and probably 33 on the Vibennii are presumably the *truces iambi* referred to at 36.5. This reference has worried editors: the phraseology seems at first sight to imply lampoons against Lesbia, which do not exist in our collection and which the poet himself claimed at one point to be incapable of writing (104). Ellis thought that the poems referred to were 8, 37 and 58; Kroll rightly excluded 8 ("das ist kein *iambus*"), but surely neither of the other two poems is appropriate either.[2] Poem 37 is indeed a lampoon, but directed against the denizens of the *salax taberna*, and in both poems the reference to Lesbia is one of sorrow rather than anger. "Quod indignum est" (37.15) is weak stuff for a Catullan invective; in fact Catullus never directly attacks Lesbia in the way he attacked the victims, male and female (cf. poem 41), of his genuine lampoons. If the arrangement of the collection is Catullus' own, however, the problem disappears: in the context of the invective sequence announced at poem 27, the reader can easily identify the "fierce iambics" as those he has just read—28, 29 and 33.

Poem 28, as we have seen, belongs after Catullus' return in 56 B.C., and poem 29 is firmly dated to 55 at the earliest; so if they are not only logically prior to 36 in the collection but also chronologically prior in order of writing—that is, if they were the *iambi* Catullus had in mind when he *wrote* 36, as well as when he arranged it in the sequence—then the poem on Volusius belongs to 55 B.C. or after.

This illuminates the question of Volusius' *Annals*. Castorino dated their publication to about 65–64 B.C., but only on the basis of the traditional Catullan chronology—and an "early" version of it at

[1] See R. Syme, *JRS* L (1960), 14 for republican Pisones, including two stray Lucii who might be our hypothetical praetor (Val. Max. VIII 1.6, Cic. *Phil.* XI 13). The father's late praetorship, and the adoption of his brother by a Pupius, may imply that that generation of Pisones was not one of outstanding prospects; this could be relevant to Cicero's marriage-alliance with them.

[2] Ellis, p. 123, Kroll, p. 67, etc. See below, p. 46 n. 2.

that.[1] He rightly pointed out the parallel between the rivers named at 95.5 and 7; but the Padua, which must be one of the mouths of the Po,[2] was surely not mentioned in order to indicate that Volusius was a Transpadane.[3] As the Satrachus was the *scene* of Cinna's poem, so the Padua must have featured in some way in Volusius' work. Baehrens suggested that Volusius' *Annals* continued those of Ennius, and dealt with the Gallic wars of the second century; but our dating of Catullus' poem makes Caesar's campaigns in Gaul a more probable subject. Furius Bibaculus' *Annals*, the projected epics of Cicero and his brother[4] and Varro Atacinus' *Bellum Sequanicum* on the campaign of 58 B.C.[5] show that they were a popular theme at the time. Catullus' disparagement of Volusius may have been as much political as literary in nature; and the point of poem 36 is perhaps enhanced if the poet's supposed farewell to political invective, which had had Caesar among its targets, as the reader knows from 29, is celebrated by the ceremonial burning of a Caesarian panegyric.

The dating of poem 36 is not only relevant to Volusius' *cacata charta*; it is of great importance for the chronology of Catullus' affair with Lesbia. But it depends, as observed above, on the assumption that 36 was *written* with the invectives of 56 and 55 B.C. in mind; it remains possible that the poem was in fact written earlier and only placed here to give coherence to the collection. Before we explore the effect of poem 36 on the Lesbia-chronology, we must try to confirm its late date.

[1] E. Castorino, *GIF* I (1948), 28–36.   [2] Polybius II 16.11, Munro, pp. 211–12.
[3] In fact, he may have been a Picene: see *CQ* XIV (1964), 126 on the Volusii, doubted by R. Syme, *Hist.* XIII (1964), 157.   [4] Cic. *QF* II 16.4, III 4.4, 5.4, 6.3, 7.6.
[5] See E. Hofmann, *WS* XLVI (1928), 172, who puts the publication of Atacinus' work *circa* 55 B.C.

V

LESBIA—WHEN?

Poem 36

Annales Volusi, cacata charta,
votum solvite pro mea puella:
nam sanctae Veneri Cupidinique
vovit, si sibi restitutus essem
desissemque truces vibrare iambos,
electissima pessimi poetae
scripta tardipedi deo daturam
infelicibus ustulanda lignis
et hoc pessima se puella vidit
iocose lepide vovere divis.   10
Nunc, o caeruleo creata ponto,
quae sanctum Idalium Uriosque apertos
quaeque Ancona Cnidumque harundinosam
colis quaeque Amathunta quaeque Golgos
quaeque Dyrrachium, Hadriae tabernam,
acceptum face redditumque votum,
si non illepidum neque invenustum est.
At vos interea venite in ignem,
pleni ruris et inficetiarum
Annales Volusi, cacata charta!   20

WHAT is the logic behind Catullus' choice of place-names
at lines 11 ff.? Idalium, Amathus and Golgi were all cult-
centres in Venus' own island of Cyprus, and Cnidos was
the home of Praxiteles' world-famous statue; but the other names
are an odd selection. There was indeed a temple of Venus at Ancona
(Juvenal IV 40), but the town was not one of the more celebrated
homes of the goddess, while "open Urii" and Dyrrachium have no
known connection with her at all. Why mention these places,
instead of (for instance) Eryx or Cythera?

The clue lies in the description of Dyrrachium as "the tavern of the sea of Hadria"—the place, that is, where travellers by sea stopped *en route* into the Adriatic. Where would such travellers go *after* Dyrrachium? The Dalmatian coast was still wild and dangerous, so the voyage would be made up the Italian side, despite the almost complete absence of good harbours north of Brundisium.[1] The Adriatic coastline of Italy is flat and alluvial, the mouths of the rivers offering protection for fishing-boats, but for nothing bigger.[2] Ancient seamen disliked such coasts; they preferred to navigate by landmarks, steering from one conspicuous promontory to the next.[3] There are only two such landmarks on the Italian Adriatic coast, the Monte Gargano peninsula in northern Apulia, and Monte Conero, the headland that shelters Ancona and gave it its Greek name[4]—and it is clear from the coastal measurements given by the ancient geographers that these were the natural landfalls for the navigators from whom their information came.[5] Ancona provides comparatively safe anchorage, but Monte Gargano has no harbours; in ancient times, however, the *lago di Varano* on the north side of the peninsula was not entirely cut off from the sea by a sand-dune, as it is now, but formed a bay which would afford some protection for shipping.[6] Evidently the present-day sand-bar had partly formed in ancient times, making the bay somewhat difficult to enter, for it must be identified as the bay at or near M. Gargano described by Mela as "*continuo Apulo litore* incinctus, nomine Urias, modicus spatio, pleraque asper accessu".[7] It was named after the town of Urium or Uria at its south-east corner, known to the Greek geographers as Ὕριον;[8] it faced north, with no protection against the

---

[1] Strabo, VII 317.   [2] Cf. H. Nissen, *Italische Landeskunde*, I (Berlin 1883), 93–4.

[3] E. C. Semple, *Geography of the Mediterranean Region* (London 1932), 584 ff.; ibid. 613 ff. on "templed promontories", including Ancona but not M. Gargano.

[4] A. Philippson, *Das Mittelmeergebiet* (Leipzig 1904), 87.

[5] Strabo, VI 285 (his sources measured the Adriatic from Brundisium to Gargano to Ancona), Pliny *NH* III 111 (Ancona "a Gargano clxxxiii"); cf. Ptol. III 1.1 and 14, *Geogr. Graeci Minores* I 22–3 (Scylax 14), II 125–6 (Dionysius *Per.* 378 ff.) on Gargano (*Hyrion* in Dionysius) as a boundary-point.

[6] It is not merely an alluvial lagoon like the nearby *lago di Lesina*: see the Touring Club Italiano guide, *Italia Meridionale*, I (Milan 1926), 551.

[7] Pomponius Mela II 4.66; identification tentatively accepted by (e.g.) Nissen, *op. cit.* II 836, 839 and G. Radke, *PW* IXA (1961), 1009–10.

[8] References in Radke, *loc. cit.* and p. 1004; Livy XLII 48.7 (four triremes *ab Uritibus*) implies a harbour. The site of the town has been located by Dr G. D. B. Jones, who

dreaded Bora, the northerly gale for which the Adriatic was notorious,[1] and thus its identification as Catullus' "Urii aperti" is practically certain.[2]

The three anomalous names in Catullus' list therefore represent the three natural stopping-places for anyone sailing from Greece to the northern end of the Adriatic—as Catullus himself did in the spring or summer of 56;[3] it is hard to resist the idea that Catullus mentioned these places in particular because he knew them himself.

From Dyrrachium to Urii is about 150 nautical miles, from Urii to Ancona about 130; each leg, that is, was about $1\frac{1}{2}$ days' sail with favourable winds, or just possibly one day for a fast boat, as Catullus' *phaselus* certainly was (4.2–5).[4] The prevailing summer winds in the Adriatic are north-west to west,[5] but south-easterlies blowing up to the head of the sea are not uncommon, and attested in ancient literature.[6] Catullus says the Adriatic was "threatening" during his voyage (4.6), but given the sea's evil reputation, the word can be taken here to indicate that the poet did *not* actually meet foul weather at this stage of his journey.[7] In any case, even if the winds were not behind her all the way, the *phaselus* was an ocean-going vessel stout enough to stay at sea for two or three days on each leg. The idea of Catullus' boat as a "puny pinnace" is exaggerated;

writes: "it lies at 667333 on no. 156 I.S.O., Lago di Varano, of the Carta d'Italia, on sloping ground between the narrow-gauge railway and the S.S. Garganica (no. 89), 3 km. N.E. of Cagnano Varano. The site must have lain almost at the water's edge in the classical period. Extent of sherds about $\frac{1}{2}$ sq. km. *in toto*—Imperial (not a lot), Republican and earlier. Passing reference to a partially exposed remain in E. Ciprioni, *Archivio Storico Pugliese* VI (1953) 278, cf. S. Ferri, *ibid.* 293."

[1] *GGM* I 212 (Scymnus 382 ff.), Hor. *Odes* I 3.15, 33.15, II 14.14, III 9.23.

[2] For the alternative, an inland Uria in Calabria, see Strabo VI 282–3, Pliny *NH* III 100. Ellis (p. 128) seems to prefer this identification, but his parallels on p. 129 for *apertus* meaning "open to the *winds*" make the Gargano port more likely. Cf. Lucan V. 378–80, Hor. *Odes* III 9.7 for the north winds blasting Gargano, and therefore Urii.

[3] Or so he tells us in poem 4: see p. 13 n. 2 above.

[4] See L. Casson's tables in *TAPA* LXXXII (1951) 136–48.

[5] Air Ministry Meteorological Office, *Weather in the Mediterranean*, II (2nd ed., London 1964), 166–71.

[6] *Ibid.* I (1962), 86 on the Adriatic *scirocco*; Hor. *Odes* I. 3.14–15 on "*Notus* arbiter Hadriae", either raising or calming the swell; cf. Livy X 2 on gales blowing a fleet *up* the Adriatic.

[7] Contrast 4.8–9; one would like to know at what point in the voyage the wind was dead astern (4.20–1). The ship made no vows to the shore-gods in bad weather (4.22–3, cf. 68.65), but the precise meaning of this passage is too uncertain to use as evidence.

Appian describes *phaseli* as a cross between merchant vessels and warships, and according to Sallust a large one could hold a cohort of soldiers.[1] They were indeed sometimes used for coasting, but also for the Adriatic crossing from Brundisium;[2] and though their range and seaworthiness may have been less than that of conventional merchantmen, we need not suppose that such craft had to creep up the Adriatic in short stages like the coasters that put in at Egnatia *en route* from Brundisium to Barium.[3]

Dyrrachium, Urii and Ancona are thus the only likely ports of call for a ship the size of the *phaselus* sailing up the Adriatic, and I think Catullus' readers were meant to recognize them as such. The allusion to the poet's journey would make Lesbia's vow look, in retrospect, like a "votum pro reditu Catulli";[4] in her capacity as Aphrodite Euploia, the name under which she was worshipped at "reedy Cnidos",[5] Venus was the protectress of sailors against shipwreck, and a very appropriate recipient for such a vow.[6] Not only the choice of these harbours among Venus' haunts, but also the use of *restitutus* in line 4 enables the reader to pick up this nuance. The poem is not *about* Catullus' journey, of course: Venus is here equally the goddess of love—of the three Cypriot cult-centres mentioned, Amathus at least was famous because of its connection with the Adonis legend[7]—and *restitutus* also means "reconciled", as at 107.4–5. But the reader alert for subtle allusion will remember poems 4 and 31—and the historian in search of chronological indications will confidently date poem 36 after Catullus' journey from Bithynia.

The "late" chronology

Nobody knows whether Lesbia *really* prayed for Catullus' safe return; the poet was quite at liberty to invent the details of his

---

[1] App. *BC* V 95, Sall. *Hist.* III 8M; cf. F. Miltner, *PW* XIX (1938), 1883–4.

[2] Cic. *Att.* XIV 16.1 (Puteoli-Pompeii), I 13.1 (Brundisium-Epirus).

[3] Strabo VI 283. See A. W. Gomme, *JHS* LIII (1933), 16–18 on merchant-ships making long hauls over the open sea.

[4] I owe this suggestion to Professor Williams.

[5] Pausanias I 1.3; cf. *CIG* 4443, 7309, 8514.

[6] *Anth. Pal.* V 11, IX 143–4, Athenaeus XV 676A ff. Hor. *Odes* III 26.5 (*Venus marina*); L. R. Farnell, *Cults of the Greek States* II (Oxford 1896), 637.

[7] Paus. IX 41.2 etc. Probably none of the three is relevant to sailors; the site of Idalium is inland, that of Golgi unknown.

relationship, and in any case, the ambiguity in this poem between the ideas of a journey's end and a reconciliation makes any precise biographical inference very hazardous. The point is worth making explicit, because (despite the traditional chronology) there is *no* other evidence that Catullus even knew Lesbia before he came back from Bithynia.[1]

More important, poem 36 shows Catullus and Lesbia on good terms—compared, for example, with the language of poem 11—in 56 B.C. at the earliest, and probably 55 if the *iambi* of line 5 included poem 29. As we have seen, these *iambi* were not directed against Lesbia: Mommsen rightly took the passage to mean that Lesbia wanted Catullus to give up political invective and spend his time and his talent on her.[2] So poem 36 implies no bitter break between them, and indeed the tone in which the implied reconciliation is treated suggests that any disagreement there may have been was a light-hearted one. That is, it is highly probable that Catullus' affair with Lesbia was in progress as late as 55 B.C.

This conclusion is of course incompatible with the traditional reconstruction of the affair (and thus of Catullus' life), which depends on the identification of Lesbia as Clodia Metelli, and places Catullus' liaison with her in the early 50s, or even the late 60s. Both the identification and the chronology have been questioned, but though editors and commentators have become more circumspect in accepting the traditional reconstruction, it remains the *communis opinio*.[3] The two questions of date and identity are usually treated as if they were one, and the attractive hypothesis that Lesbia was the Clodia of the *pro Caelio* has predisposed scholars in favour of the

---

[1] Catullus speaks of a "longus amor" at 76.13, but by Roman standards this could be anything longer than a few weeks (cf. Quinn, pp. 74 ff.)—besides, poem 76 is itself undateable.

Nor do we know how soon after his return Catullus wrote poem 36. The reader is expected to know about Catullus' journey, but this need not mean that the poem was written so soon after his return that he *must* have known Lesbia before he left. If poems 4 and 31 had already been circulated, Catullus could surely have counted on his readers' recognition of the allusions long after the event—certainly long enough after for him to have fallen in love with Lesbia in the meantime.

[2] T. Mommsen, *History of Rome* (Everyman trans., London 1911), IV, 550-1. Whichever one of P. Clodius' sisters Lesbia was (see ch. VI), such a request is quite comprehensible after April 56, when Clodius was persuaded to support the "triumvirs".

[3] e.g. Quinn, p. 113 n. 4: "this has been doubted, but it seems tolerably certain".

early chronology. I propose to separate the two problems, and leave the identification of Lesbia until the chronological probabilities become more clear.

The main argument against the traditional chronology is that no poem can be dated earlier than 56–55 B.C. on internal evidence. Poems 11, 29, 45, 52, 55, 84 and 113 belong to 55 B.C. or later;[1] 4, 10, 31 and 46 are dated to 56 B.C. by Memmius' proconsulship of Bithynia. Rothstein, the first serious opponent of the traditional chronology, claimed that no fewer than thirty-one poems certainly belonged to these years.[2] He achieved this total by adding poems 101 (on the brother's death) and 9, 12 and 28 (on Veranius and Fabullus) to the group of poems about Catullus' return from Bithynia in 56 B.C.; to the "55" group he added poems 54 ("unice imperator", like 29.11), 41, 43 and 57 (Mamurra), 15, 16, 21, 23, 24, 26, 48, 81 and 99 (Furius, Aurelius, Juventius), and 5 and 7 (because of 16.12); finally, identifying the Cominius of 108 with the prosecutor of C. Cornelius in 65, he put the poem at the end of Catullus' life on the strength of "cana senectus" in line 1. Some of these attributions are certainly unjustifiable, notably 101 (see p. 37 above), and 5 and 7 (written *how long* before 16?), and it is certainly stretching the evidence to make the whole of the Furius-Aurelius-Juventius cycle necessarily contemporary with poem 11. But he was probably right, as we have seen above, to make the journey of Veranius and Fabullus to Spain contemporary with that of Catullus to Bithynia. Rothstein's "thirty-one" poems should be reduced to about fourteen, to which we can now add poem 36; but even so, fifteen out of 116 poems dateable to two consecutive years, and not a single one inconsistent with that dating, make a very powerful *prima facie* case against placing the undateable poems up to five years earlier.

Rothstein confused his own case, however, by dating "poem 68" very early, to about 64 B.C., on the strength of lines 15–20 which he believed must have been written not long after Catullus took the *toga virilis*. This involved him in two very difficult hypotheses: that "poem 68" was not about Lesbia, and that Catullus had already been

---

[1] We can surely add poem 53: see E. S. Gruen, *HSCP* LXXI (1966), 217–21, who argues strongly for 54 as the date of Calvus' *only* prosecution of Vatinius. 54 would also be a most appropriate time to call Cicero "omnium patronus" (poem 49): see *JRS* LVI (1966), 109 and Gruen *loc. cit.* 219 ff.

[2] Rothstein, pp. 30–2, etc.

writing poetry in the 60s but had kept only the long poems written at that time (e.g. 68), and destroyed, lost or suppressed the short ones.[1]

This unnecessary complication was abandoned by Maas, the other opponent of the orthodox chronology, who took the passage from 68 in the opposite sense: "a writer who speaks in these terms of the time when he got the *toga virilis* is likely to be nearer his thirtieth year (according to the new chronology) than his twenty-fifth (according to the old)".[2] Such precision is hardly justified, but Maas was right to correct Rothstein's view;[3] he considered that *all* the poems belong after Catullus' Bithynian journey, and that "his literary career began in 56 B.C.". Like Rothstein, Maas made poem 43 on Mamurra's mistress contemporary with poem 29 on Mamurra (i.e. in or after 55 B.C.); "tecum Lesbia nostra comparatur" (43.7) thus indicates friendly relations between Catullus and Lesbia at a period hardly possible on the orthodox timetable. Maas also dated poems 36 and 37 late, and drew the same conclusion from them, though his inference of a "period of harmony" from poem 37 (based on the parallels of 37.11/11.17 and 37.12/8.5) is tenuous in the extreme. Poem 36 he also put late because of a verbal parallel— 36.18 with 14.21, which he connected with the poems on Vatinius (52 and 53) written in 55 or 54 B.C.[4] This too is tenuous, but we can now confirm the late dating of 36 on other grounds.

In short, the two opponents of the traditional chronology used arguments of very unequal value, and differed from each other on points of detail. But tenuous inferences notwithstanding, the fact remains that the basis of their heretical view is perfectly sound: other things being equal, the collection should be dated to 56/54 B.C.

But are the other things equal? The traditional chronology is based largely on the identification of Lesbia with Clodia Metelli, and thus of Caelius and/or Rufus (poems 58, 100, 69, 77) with her lover M. Caelius Rufus. Realizing this, Rothstein made the supposedly superior claims of Clodia Luculli a major part of his case for

---

[1] Rothstein, pp. 9 ff., 30. This, with Rothstein's dating of 101, implies that Catullus visited his brother's tomb nearly ten years after the latter's death.

[2] Maas, p. 80, etc.

[3] He was also right (p. 79) to detach poem 101 from the Bithynian journey.

[4] Maas, p. 81.

redating; Maas, on the other hand, evidently thought that Lesbia could still be Metellus' wife (or rather widow) on the late chronology.[1] The question arises whether Lesbia *can* be identified, and if so, whether the identification requires a date for Catullus' poems different from the one suggested by internal evidence.

[1] Rothstein, pp. 19 ff.; cf. Maas, pp. 80, 81.

VI

LESBIA—WHO?

The evidence of Apuleius

Eadem opera accusent C. Catullum quod Lesbiam pro Clodia nominarit, et Ticidam similiter quod quae Metella erat Perillam scripserit, et Propertium qui Cynthiam dicat Hostiam dissimulet, et Tibullum quod ei sit Plania in anima, Delia in versu.

(Apuleius, Apology 10)

THERE is no reason to disbelieve Apuleius' testimony, especially as it is consistent with the Latin poets' supposed habit of making pseudonyms metrically equivalent to the names disguised.[1] But it is worth asking where Apuleius, writing over two centuries after the event, got his information from.

Like his archaizing contemporaries Fronto and Gellius, Apuleius was well acquainted with the life and literature of the late Republic. His thorough knowledge of Cicero is attested by his list of accusations *gloriae causa*, his assessment of the great republican orators, and other passages in the *Apology*.[2] He quotes Varro on magic and divination, and wrote a *de re rustica* which may have been derived from Varro;[3] he was knowledgeable about early Roman law[4] and was aware of the existence of a *collegium* of Isis-worshippers in Rome at the time of Sulla.[5] As for republican poetry, his *Apology*, *Florida* and *de deo Socratis* contain quotations from Ennius, Accius, Plautus, Terence, Laevius, Afranius, Lucilius, Aedituus, Porcius, Catulus, Lucretius, Catullus and two unknown poets.[6] But what

---

[1] Ps. Acro on Hor. *Sat.* I. 2.64: "eodem numero syllabarum commutationem facit, ut Licymniam Malchinum Villium pro Terentia Maecenate Annio".

[2] Apul. *apol.* 66, 95, cf. 17, 20; R. Helm, *Apuleius* (Teubner, Leipzig 1959), vol. II fasc. 2, pp. xxii–xxviii.

[3] *Apol.* 42—from Varro's *Curio de cultu deorum* (Aug, *CD* VII 35), which evidently dealt with hydromancy etc.: B. Cardauns, *Varros Logistoricus über die Götterverehrung*, (Würzburg 1960), 31–2, 45–50. *De re rustica*: Photius *bibl.* 163, Palladius I 35.9.

[4] Helm *op. cit.* xii f; e.g. *Met.* VIII 24 on the *lex Cornelia*.　　[5] *Met.* XI 30 *ad fin.*

[6] Catullus: *Apol.* 6, 11, cf. 10, 16 "albus an ater". Others: *Apol.* 9, 10, 12, 30, 39, 58, *Florida* 2, 10, 18, 21, 23, *deo Socr.* 1, 2, 5, 10, 20.

was his source for the passage in question on the disguised mistresses of famous poets?

One clue comes from the Byzantine Johannes Lydus' work *de magistratibus*, which quotes two authorities on the love of Sandon, an Anatolian god equated with Hercules, for Omphale: they are "Apuleius the Roman philosopher in the book entitled *Eroticus*, and before him Tranquillus in his work *On Famous Prostitutes*".[1] Tranquillus is Suetonius, so Apuleius' otherwise unknown *Eroticus* may have used Suetonius' *de scortis illustribus*. But even if the poets' mistresses counted as *scorta* for Suetonius (and he may equally have mentioned them in his *de poetis*), this only takes us one generation back. How did Suetonius know? Fortunately, we know from the preface to Jerome's *de viris illustribus* the sources Suetonius probably used for his biographical works: they were Varro, Santra, Nepos and Hyginus.[2] Nepos, who was a friend of Catullus,[3] and Varro, who wrote a *de poetis* and whose *Menippean Satires* Catullus had surely read before he wrote poem 63,[4] might both have known who Lesbia was, but could hardly have lived to discuss the identification of Propertius' and Tibullus' mistresses. The same probably applies to their contemporary Santra.[5]

We are left with C. Julius Hyginus, the polymath who succeeded Varro as director of the Palatine library. His work *de vita rebusque illustrium virorum* was no doubt what Suetonius used, as did Gellius,[6] but he wrote many other things besides. Suetonius tells us that he was a friend of Ovid, and it is hard to see to whom else Ovid could have addressed letter 14 in the third book of his *Tristia*, which begins "cultor et antistes doctorum sancte virorum . . ." This letter is important for our purpose, because its recipient is also described as "vatum studiose *novorum*";[7] Hyginus wrote on Vergil, and indeed

---

[1] Lyd. *mag.* III 64 (155 Wuensch) on the σάνδυξ, a Lydian women's garment also known as "Heracles' tunic".

[2] J.-P. Migne, *Patrologiae*, Series Latina XXIII (Paris 1883), 361.

[3] Cat. 1, Nep. *Att.* 12.

[4] Varro *Men.* 79, 131–3, 364 (Buecheler); dated to the eighties and seventies B.C. by C. Cichorius, *Römische Studien* (Leipzig 1922), 207–26.

[5] H. Dahlmann, in *PW* Supp. VI (1935), 1178, suggests that Varro's *de poetis* was written about 47 B.C. For Santra, who is quoted on nothing later than the Atticist controversy (Quint. XII 10.16), see Schanz-Hosius, *Gesch. der röm. Literatur* (München 1927), I 584.

[6] Gell. I 14.1, VI 1.2, III 4.1.   [7] Suet. *gramm.* 20, Ovid *Trist.* III 14.1 and 7.

was "almost his tutor" according to Columella, but a reference to his commentary on Cinna's *propempticon Pollionis* shows that he did not restrict himself to the Augustans.[1] A better candidate for Apuleius' source on Lesbia, Perilla, Cynthia and Delia it would be difficult to find, particularly as the only other reference to the pseudonymity of Lesbia and Perilla comes from Hyginus' friend Ovid himself.[2]

Hyginus probably came to Rome in 47 B.C.[3] Catullus was almost certainly dead by then, but Cinna, Cornificius or Pollio (not to mention Nepos, Varro and perhaps Cicero) could have told him who Lesbia was. Besides, there was at least one Clodia alive at the time—the woman whose gardens Cicero was thinking of buying in 45 B.C.[4]—so Hyginus might even have got his information from Lesbia herself, or from her sister.

The incest charge

This brings us to the question, to which Clodia Apuleius' source was referring. We can narrow it down to one of the sisters of Ap. Claudius Pulcher (*cos.* 54) and P. Clodius Pulcher (*tr. pl.* 58) with the help of Catullus' poem 79:

> Lesbius est pulcher: quid ni? quem Lesbia malit
> quam te cum tota gente, Catulle, tua.
> Sed tamen hic pulcher vendat cum gente Catullum
> si tria notorum savia reppererit.

The pun on the name Clodius *Pulcher* is unmistakable.[5] Besides, the incestuous relations imputed between Lesbius and Lesbia agree with P. Clodius' supposed incest with his sisters. He had three sisters: the youngest was married to L. Licinius Lucullus but divorced in

---

[1] Gellius I 21.2, X 16.1 etc. (Columella I 1.13); Charisius 134K.

[2] Ovid *Trist.* II 428 ("femina cui falsum Lesbia nomen erat") and 437–8 ("modo dissimulata Perillae nomine, nunc legitur dicta, Metelle, tuo").

[3] Suet. *gramm.* 20.

[4] Cic. *Att.* XII 38a.2—XIII 29.2 (perhaps Metellus Celer's widow: *Cael.* 36 for her riverside *horti*). *Att.* XI 6.3, 9.2 for a Clodia in 49 (mother-in-law of L. Metellus), who might be the same woman.

[5] G. Giri, in *RIGI* VI (1922), 12–15, tried to equate Lesbius with "Sex. Clodius"; the suggestions of *irrumatio* (or *fellatio*) at 79.4 and in Cic. *Cael.* 78, *dom.* 25, 47, 83 and *har. resp.* 11 made this suggestion attractive, but it was disproved when D. R. Shackleton Bailey showed that "Sex. Clodius" was really Sex. Cloelius: *CQ* LIV (1960), 41–2.

66 B.C.; Tertia, presumably the third daughter born but either the first or second to survive, was married to Q. Marcius Rex but widowed by 61 B.C.; the other, older than Clodius himself and possibly the eldest of the three sisters, was married to Q. Metellus Celer but widowed in 59 B.C.[1] The evidence for Clodius' supposed relations with each of these must be examined carefully, and in chronological order.

(i) In 68 B.C. Clodius was serving under his brother-in-law Lucullus in Asia, and was supposed to have incited a mutiny in his army; describing Clodius' character in this context, Plutarch says that he was accused of seducing his sister, Lucullus' wife. (ii) In his account of Lucullus' divorce of Clodia after his return and triumph in 66, Plutarch mentions "the scandal about her brothers" as one of Clodia's bad features.[2] Neither of these comments is chronologically reliable; probably both anticipate the event described in the next references.

(iii) At Clodius' trial for sacrilege early in 61 B.C., according to Plutarch's life of Caesar, "the most powerful of the senators" bore witness that he had committed adultery with his sister when she was Lucullus' wife. (iv) In his biography of Cicero, Plutarch expands this report and specifies that Lucullus himself produced slave-girls who testified to this effect; there was also a "general belief" that Clodius had incestuous relations with his other two sisters, rumour being particularly strong about Clodia Metelli.[3] (v) Welcome confirmation of the evidence given at the trial comes from Cicero, speaking in 52 B.C. about Clodius, "quem cum sorore germana nefarium stuprum fecisse L. Lucullus iuratus se quaestionibus habitis dixit comperisse" (*Mil.* 73).

(vi) Some fifteen months after his trial, when Metellus Celer was consul, Clodius complained that his sister Clodia Metelli wouldn't give him and his clients a single foot of seating space at the gladiatorial games. "Noli", answered Cicero, "de uno pede sororis queri; licet etiam alterum tollas."[4] Cicero admitted in the next sentence

---

[1] Plut. *Cic.* 29.3 on the youngest, Cic. *Cael.* 36 on Clodius' "maior soror". In *Lat.* XXIV (1965) 60, I rashly followed F. Münzer (*Römische Adelsparteien* (Stuttgart 1920), 351–2), who supposed Tertia to be the youngest.

[2] Plut. *Luc.* 34.1 ἦν καὶ διαφθείρειν ἔσχεν αἰτίαν, 38.1 ἡ τῶν ἀδελφῶν διαβολή.

[3] Plut. *Caes.* 10.5, *Cic.* 29.3–4—πολλὴ δ' ἦν δόξα . . . .

[4] Cic. *Att.* II 1.5 (June 60).

that he hated the woman, and his jibe cannot be taken as reliable evidence. Sworn testimony about Clodia Luculli had been given in open court not much more than a year before; this was enough for Cicero to make insinuations about Metellus' wife, particularly as "de uno pede sororis" could refer to either. It is clearly an example of Clodius' "bad reputation" about his other two sisters which resulted, as Plutarch observes, from the disclosures about the youngest—and, we may add, from Cicero's hostility to Clodia Metelli.

(vii) The same may be said of Cicero's reference to Clodius as "sororicida" in the *de domo sua* (September 29th, 57 B.C.); "sororem tuam", he goes on, "virginem esse non sisti", thus suggesting that Clodius' incestuous relations had begun before the sister concerned was married, but again leaving it ambiguous which sister he meant.[1]

(viii) In the *pro Sestio* (February 10th, 56), Clodius is "sororiis stupris, omni inaudita libidine exsanguis . . . scurrarum locupletium scortum, sororis adulter, stuprorum sacerdos . . . qui omnia sororis embolia novit". We are still not told *which* sister, though the audience at the trial must have got Cicero's meaning, if they were the same people who shouted obscene rhymes "in Clodium et Clodiam" a few weeks later; Cicero, writing to his brother about the latter occasion, seems to be talking about Metellus' widow.[2]

(ix) There is no doubt which Clodia is referred to in the *pro Caelio* (April 4th, 56), but Cicero's treatment of her relations with Clodius remains on the level of mocking insinuation without proof or evidence: "cum istius mulieris viro—fratrem volui dicere, semper hic erro . . . [Clodius] qui te amat plurimum, qui propter nescio quam, credo, timiditatem et nocturnos quosdam inanis metus tecum semper pusio cum maiore sorore cubitabat . . . eadem mulier cum suo coniuge et fratre . . ." At one point he even confirms the "hearsay" nature of the charge—so far as Clodia Metelli was concerned—when he observes that Caelius, as her neighbour, could hardly help being talked about in connection with a woman "cuius frater germanus *sermones iniquorum* effugere non potuit".[3]

(x) In the *de haruspicum responso* (May or September, 56 B.C.), there is one apparent allusion to Clodia Metelli in Clodius' fondness for

---

[1] Cic. *dom.* 96—also *fratricida*!   [2] Cic. *Sest.* 16, 39, 116; *QF* II 3.2.
[3] Cic. *Cael.* 32, 36, 78; 38.

the "blazing eyes" of his sister, but the other relevant passages are the same familiar vague generalities: "[Clodius] qui post patris mortem primam illam aetatulam suam ad scurrarum locupletium libidinis detulit, quorum intemperantia expleta in domesticis et germanitatis stupris volutatus est . . . quis umquam nepos tam libere est cum scortis quam hic cum sororibus volutatus?" Cicero has now extended his charge to include more than one sister, but he still does not specify which he means.[1] (xi) Finally, his attack on Piso (summer 55) includes a reference to "ille sororius adulter", and in his long public letter to Lentulus Spinther in December 54 he observes that Clodius "non pluris fecerat Bonam Deam quam tris sorores".[2]

From this body of evidence we gather that Clodius had a bad sexual reputation in his youth,[3] that he was known to have committed incest with his youngest sister when she was still Lucullus' wife (i.e. before 66), that after this came to light at his trial in 61 his *inimici* exploited it by suggesting that he habitually had relations with all three sisters,[4] and that Cicero in particular directed this slander against Clodia Metelli, whom (on his own admission) he detested. So if poem 79 were a reliable document of historical fact, we could say firmly that Lesbia was Clodia Luculli and no other. Unfortunately, it is not as simple as that. Poem 79 is as malicious— and therefore perhaps as baseless—an invective as those of Cicero and the Forum crowd about Clodia Metelli. It could quite conceivably be about the same woman.

Caelius Rufus and the missing husband

But if the "Lesbius" poem cannot prove that Lesbia was Clodia Luculli, still less can it prove that she was either of the other sisters; as Rothstein observes, it is fruitless to attempt a "judgement of Paris" between them. However, the history of the reputation of Clodius and his sisters is useful in that it exposes the sort of specious argument sometimes put forward in favour of Lesbia being Clodia Metelli—that since both women were beautiful, clever, cultured,

---

[1] Cic. *har. resp.* 38 (cf. *Cael.* 49), 42, 59.

[2] Cic. *Pis.* 28, *Fam.* I 9.15.

[3] Inferred from the direction of Cicero's attacks at *dom.* 92, *har. resp.* 42, *Sest.* 39 and *Cael.* 36 ("semper . . . cubitabat").

[4] And his brothers: Cic. *dom.* 92, cf. Plut. *Luc.* 38.1.

E

aristocratic, married to stupid husbands, unfaithful, corrupt and eventually degraded to the point of prostitution, therefore they are identical. Even if it could be proved that Metellus Celer was particularly stupid, this would not be enough to equate him with the *fatuus mulus* of poem 83: the description of a woman's husband by her lover is hardly likely to be disinterested. Even if poems 37 and 58 could be taken as meaning that Lesbia had literally sunk to the level of a common whore, this would not be enough to equate her with the Clodia of the *pro Caelio*: since Cicero had his own forensic reasons to make out that Clodia was a *meretrix*—to exculpate Caelius' relations with her, and to impugn the validity of her evidence[1]—we should not lightly believe him either. As for the other supposed points of similarity, they apply to any of the three sisters, and to many other Roman noblewomen besides.[2] If we had a speech against Clodius from 61 B.C. instead of one in defence of Caelius from 56, the identification of Clodia Luculli as Lesbia would seem as self-evident as that of Clodia Metelli has appeared to many modern scholars.

Clodia Metelli was the mistress of M. Caelius Rufus from some time after her husband died in 59 B.C. until some time before Caelius' trial in April 56.[3] The identification of Caelius Rufus as the Rufus of poems 69 and 77 and/or the Caelius of poems 58 and 100 is another apparent argument for the identity of this Clodia and Lesbia which collapses at close inspection. Catullus' Caelius was a Veronese; M. Caelius Rufus came from Interamnia Praetuttiorum.[4] Catullus' Caelius was a trusted friend and confidant of the poet in his affair with Lesbia; Catullus' Rufus was a treacherous rival, one of Lesbia's lovers. The possibility remains that Catullus' Rufus was M. Caelius Rufus, but the *cognomen* is so infinitely common that without confirmation—and there is none—nothing can be built on this supposition.[5]

---

[1] T. A. Dorey, *GR* V (1958), 175 ff., esp. 178 n. 3.

[2] Cf. Rothstein, p. 9, quoting Ovid *AA* I 59: "quot caelum stellas, tot habet tua Roma puellas"! *Ibid.* 20 for the judgement of Paris; Giri, *loc. cit.* (p. 52 n. 5 above) 2–10, refutes all the supposed similarities at length.

[3] As Giri points out elsewhere (*Ath.* 1928, 217–18), there is nothing in the *pro Caelio* to suggest that Clodia was unfaithful to Metellus while he was alive; however, Cicero seems to refer to a lover (Fabius) at *Att.* II 1.5 *ad fin.* (cf. Shackleton Bailey, *ad loc.*).   [4] 100.2, Cic. *Cael.* 5.

[5] Giri, *loc. cit.* 10–11; Rothstein, pp. 15–18 and *Phil.* LXXXI (1926), 472; Maas, p. 81.

The main argument in favour of Clodia Metelli is that she is known to have been married at a time supposedly within the period when Catullus' poems were written. She was widowed early in 59 B.C., whereas her youngest sister had been divorced in 66 and the third widowed by 61 at the latest.[1] Since Catullus refers to Lesbia's *vir* in poems 68b and 83, we evidently have to look for a married woman rather than a widow or a divorcee. But, as we have seen, there is no reason except the very identification in question to suppose that any of Catullus' poems were written before 56 B.C. Rothstein and Maas, who rightly insist on the late chronology, suppose that *vir* does not mean "husband" but "recognized lover".[2] This is certainly possible in poem 83, but it is utterly incredible in the carefully worked-out marriage imagery of 68b, where Lesbia's *adultery* with Catullus is central to the entire poem.[3] There *must* have been a husband.

The dilemma may be set out as follows:

(*a*) Lesbia was one of the three Clodiae.
(*b*) Lesbia was married.
(*c*) Catullus' poems, including those on Lesbia, were written *c.* 56–54 B.C.
(*d*) None of the Clodiae was married at that time.

At least one of these propositions must be false. Giri denied (*a*), but his treatment of poem 79 was based on an unsound premise;[4] Rothstein and Maas denied (*b*), but only by making nonsense of poem 68b. The traditional reconstruction implies the denial of (*c*), but poem 36 shows clearly enough that the early stages of the poet's relationship with Lesbia do not have to be put before the trip to Bithynia.[5] Rather than go against the consistent chronological indications of the fifteen poems which can be internally dated, I should prefer to deny (*d*).

Whichever one of the sisters Lesbia was, she was the daughter of Ap. Claudius Pulcher and Metella, and therefore descended from

[1] Cic. *Att.* I 16.10 (July? 61) on Q. Marcius Rex' will.
[2] Rothstein, pp. 24–9. Maas, p. 81 (Rothstein not concerned with poem 68—see p. 47 above); cf. Cic. *Cael.* 38 "palam decretum semper aliquem", Ovid *AA* II 597, etc. for *vir* in this sense.
[3] See pp. 22–4 above.
[4] See p. 52 n. 5 above.
[5] Also poem 43? Cf. Maas, p. 81.

two great noble families who were accustomed to employ their womenfolk to good political effect in dynastic marriages;[1] she had herself been given in marriage to a great politician (all the Clodiae had consular husbands), and since her own family lacked the funds to match their ambition,[2] it is hard to imagine her and her sisters being left unproductively single for very long after death and divorce had sundered them from Lucullus, Marcius Rex and Metellus Celer. The marital careers of her cousins and contemporaries show us what to expect. Mucia Tertia, divorced by Pompey late in 62 B.C., was married to M. Scaurus by 54 at the latest, and probably much earlier; Sulla's daughter Fausta evidently married Milo in 55 almost immediately after her divorce from C. Memmius; Cornelia, the daughter of Metellus Scipio, was married to young P. Crassus in 55 B.C., widowed in 53 by the battle of Carrhae, and remarried to Pompey early in 52.[3] Lesbia's sister-in-law Fulvia, widowed by Clodius' murder in 52, married Curio immediately afterwards, and then Antony after Curio was killed in Africa in 49.[4] At an only slightly lower social level we find Cornificia, sister of one of Catullus' friends and eventually married to another, described in 45 B.C. as "vetula sane et *multarum nuptiarum*"; herself of praetorian family, she refused a further offer of marriage from the *nobilis* M. Juventius Thalna.[5] In the next generation there are Scribonia, married to two consulars in succession and then to Octavian; her successor Livia Drusilla, divorced and remarried while still carrying her first husband's child; and her daughter Julia, married to Marcellus but widowed in 23, remarried to Agrippa in 21 but widowed again in 12 B.C., and finally married to Tiberius the following year.[6]

---

[1] Cf. R. Syme, *Roman Revolution* (Oxford 1939), 20, 43 on the women of the Metelli; I have tried to pursue the subject in *Lat.* XXIV (1965), 52 ff. [2] Varro *RR* III 16.2.

[3] Asc. 19C "nam Tertiam Scaevolae filiam dimissam a Pompeio in matrimonium duxerat" (*sc.* Scaurus—their son was an active legate by 35: App. *BC* V 142); *ibid.* 28C "T. Annius Milo, cui Fausta ante paucos menses nupserat dimissa a Memmio"; Plut. *Pomp.* 55.1, etc. on Cornelia.

[4] Cic. *Phil.* II 11 for Curio, who had been a friend of Clodius in 61.

[5] Cic. *Att.* XIII 29.1, *CIL* I² 793: Cornificia Q.f. Cameri (cf. Cat. 55). See F. Münzer, *PW* IV (1900), 1631: she was also a poetess (Jer. *Chron.* 1976 Abr.). Thalna too had been a friend of Clodius (Cic. *Att.* I 16.6), and is identified by Shackleton Bailey with Catullus' Juventius.

[6] Suet. *DA* 62–3; cf. Syme, *op. cit.* 229 n. 7 on Scribonia. The implication of Val. Max. IV 3.3 on Antonia Drusi is that prolonged widowhood was unusual: cf. also Jos. *AJ* XVIII 180.

"The *nobiles* were dynasts, their daughters princesses. . . ."[1] What is surprising is not the notion that the Clodiae might have remarried, but the fact that Clodia Metelli had evidently not yet done so at the time of the *pro Caelio*, three years after Metellus Celer's death. Family loyalty, always strong among the Claudii,[2] must have required the Clodiae to seek second marriages; and though their unsavoury reputations (however undeserved in two out of the three cases) might have made them unattractive to their aristocratic equals, there were many influential men of slightly lesser degree who would be flattered by such a marriage and who could be useful for the political fortunes of the family.

Such a one, perhaps, was the *eques* A. Ofilius, an intimate friend of Caesar and mentioned by Cicero in 45 B.C. in the company of Caesar's powerful aide, L. Balbus.[3] The most learned jurist of his day, he was a pupil of Ser. Sulpicius Rufus, whose family was well known in the circles frequented by Clodius and his sisters (and Catullus);[4] either he or his father may have been the heir of Sempronius Tuditanus, the grandfather of Clodius' wife Fulvia.[5] By pure chance, we happen to know that he was married to a Clodia; she was remembered for having borne fifteen children and died at the age of 115.[6] She is mentioned with Livia Rutili and Terentia Ciceronis, and was therefore surely a woman of some standing. Münzer thought she might be a cousin or niece of the three sisters,[7] but the spelling of the name counts against this if Suetonius was right to call Clodius' daughter Claudia.[8] No woman of the family is known to have spelt her name in this way except the three sisters,[9] and it is quite conceivable that Ofilius' wife could have been one of them.

To sum up: there is no reason—to put it at its weakest—to suppose that Lesbia and her sisters had not remarried by the period

[1] Syme, *op. cit.* 12.
[2] For their solidarity in the mid-fifties, cf. Cic. *Att.* IV 3.4, *Cael.* 55 ("ex inimica . . . domo"), *QF* II 12.2, etc. Perhaps a hint of it at Cat. 79.2–3?
[3] Pomp. *Dig.* I 2.2.44, Cic. *Att.* XIII 37.4.   [4] *CQ* XVIII (1968) 301f.
[5] Val. Max. VII 8.1, where Lipsius read "(O)filium".
[6] Val. Max. VIII 3.16, Pliny *NH* VII 158.   [7] F. Münzer, *PW* XVII (1937), 2040.
[8] Suet. *DA* 62; *ILS* 882 for her brother (but cf. Cic. *Att.* XIV 13a.2).
[9] Cic. *Att.* XII 22.2 (cf. *CQ* XVIII (1968) 300) for a Clodia two generations earlier —probably a Marcella.

56–54 B.C. when the dateable poems of Catullus were written. There is therefore no reason to date the rest of his poems any earlier on the strength of the one-in-three chance that Lesbia was Clodia Metelli. Catullus may well have known M. Caelius Rufus, though whether he attacked him in poems 69 and 77 it is impossible to say. It is unlikely that he ever knew Metellus Celer; that worthy man was surely in his tomb when Catullus loved the woman who was either his widow or one of his sometime sisters-in-law. The love affair between Catullus and Clodia took place—so far as the evidence allows us to know—in the period after Catullus' return from Bithynia in 56 B.C.

It is over a century since Ludwig Schwabe published his *Quaestiones Catullianae* (Giessen 1862), in which the traditional chronology of Catullus' life and writings was first constructed. Schwabe's theory has had a long innings—longer perhaps than its factual basis deserved. Can we now be rid of it at last?

Index of Catullan passages

Index of persons